# THE CORN COOK BOOK

# *The*
# Corn
# Cook Book

## [WAR EDITION]

*Compiled and Arranged by*

## Elizabeth O. Hiller

**Formerly Principal of the Chicago Domestic
Science Training School, Lecturer
on Household Economics**

## Creative Cook Book
## Monterey, California

The Corn Cook Book

Compiled and Arranged by
Elizabeth O. Hiller

ISBN 1-58963-122-6

# Preface

"Save the wheat" is the call that has been sent out from Washington to the housekeepers of America.

In response to this urgent plea, this new War Edition of the Corn Cook Book containing 200 recipes has been compiled, showing the various ways that this valuable cereal can be utilized so as to save wheat for ourselves and our Allies.

Corn is the American Indian's greatest gift to civilization. The early colonists used it to a large extent. It is still one of the most important and delectable foods of the South and the New England States. No one who has tasted the real Southern Corn Pone will ever forget its deliciousness.

This book includes many substantial, inexpensive dishes made from corn, some of which are unusually attractive in appearance as well as taste. Each recipe has been carefully tested and will produce satisfactory results if the instructions given in the chapter on Measuring and Combining Ingredients are faithfully followed.

These simple, palatable, wholesome dishes will lend great variety to the daily menus and enable the housewife to utilize at the lowest possible cost the cereal which ranks in food value with wheat.

To the housewives of America the author dedicates this little volume "The Corn Cook Book" with the earnest hope that it will do its part towards winning the war by helping to conserve the Nation's Food.

Faithfully yours,

Mrs. Elizabeth O. Hiller.

# How to Measure Ingredients

It is absolutely necessary to measure all ingredients correctly to insure success in cooking.

Satisfactory results have been attained, occasionally, by those of long experience and good judgment in measuring by sight; but when failures are made, discouragement follows and, too, habits of wastefulness are acquired by this "hit or miss" method. The majority of people need a definite system of measurements which, when carefully followed, must yield satisfactory results. Granite measuring cups, divided in thirds and quarters, holding one-half pint, table and teaspoons of regulation size, a common case knife, all of which may be purchased at any kitchen furnishing store, are among the essential articles for measuring correctly. Flour, meal, powdered sugar, soda, mustard, ginger, baking powder, and all ingredients which stand in boxes, settle and sometimes harden in lumps, should be crushed and sifted before measuring. A cupful is a half-pint cup filled, and leveled with a knife.

### To fill a measuring cup, a table or teaspoon

Toss the dry ingredients lightly into a measuring cup, heap it slightly, and level it with a knife. Shortening, such as butter, lard and other fats, are packed solidly into both cup and spoon, and leveled with a knife. A tablespoon is measured level. A teaspoon is measured level.

In measuring with either tea or tablespoon, dip the spoon into the material, fill it, lift, and level with a case knife, turning sharp edge of blade toward handle of spoon. Divide with the knife, lengthwise of bowl of spoon for a half, divide the half crosswise for a quarter and the quarter crosswise for an eighth. When less than an eighth is called for use a few grains. A tablespoon of correct size should hold three level teaspoons. A teaspoon should hold sixty drops of liquid.

## Measuring Liquids

A cup of liquid is an even cupful or all the cup will hold. Tablespoon and teaspoonful is all the spoon will hold. When the following ingredients are called for in a recipe, measure the dry, fats and liquids in the order given, thereby making one cup serve the purpose of all.

## To Combine Mixtures

Use an earthen mixing bowl of ample size for mixing batters and doughs. Mix with a wooden spoon. Measure all ingredients correctly; mix and sift the flour, baking powder, spices, etc., before measuring.

Count out the desired number of eggs, selecting those of uniform size, especially if a cake is to be made. Break each egg separately over a cup; that there may be no loss should a stale one chance to be one of the number.

Separate the whites from the yolks when so specified. Eggs are beaten three degrees of lightness. They are "slightly beaten" when whites and yolks, beaten together, will run from the tines of a fork. They are "lightly beaten," when beaten thick, very light and a lemon tint.

Whites are beaten alone stiff and dry.

Measure butter and liquid as suggested in the foregoing. Having everything in readiness, the mixing and baking of these mixtures may be quickly done.

## TIMELY SUGGESTIONS

The milk called for in the recipes incorporated in this book is skimmed milk, except where cream is called for and in such recipes the finished product will serve as the main dish for breakfast, luncheon or supper.

**Milk** should always be heated or scalded over hot water. Milk is seldom boiled in modern cookery. Occasionally "boiled milk" is found in Sick Room Cookery.

Water should be boiling rapidly when cereals are added. Corn meal and granulated hominy will combine with boiling water more readily if it is first moistened with some of the water before water is set to boil. Mush and porridges of all kinds are better seasoned if the seasoning is added to the boiling water, before adding the meal or cereal.

Long, slow cooking develops the flavor of corn meal and hominy and aids materially the process of digestion.

When preparing mush for frying, part milk should form part of the liquid or wetting to insure a rich brown crisp surface when finished. Mush to be sliced for frying etc., should never be packed in either tin or Russia iron bread pans as the salt and moisture will cause rust to form and settle on the mush and when turned from pan these spots look unsightly. A brick-shaped agate bread pan is best for this purpose or Pyrex glass bread pans.

Lightly grease the knife used for slicing cold mush; it will cut more evenly without breaking.

Tried out salt pork fat is the best fat to use for sauteing purposes as it burns at a very high temperature, This is especially true of butter. The vegetable oils give very satisfactory results both for deep frying and sauteing.

Corn meal and all cereals should be kept in a cool, dry place. The "water milled" corn meal from which nothing is removed makes the best flavored pone, dodgers, mush and in fact all the quick breads usually made from corn meal.

This (Water Milled) corn meal has not the keeping qualities that the modern commercial corn meals have. It should therefore be purchased in smaller quantities and used at once.

# MOTIONS USED IN MIXING INGREDIENTS

Three motions are considered in mixing batters, doughs and other ingredients, namely: stirring, beating, cutting and folding.

STIRRING is a rotary motion ordinarily used in all cookery. It is to thoroughly mix the ingredients.

BEATING is turning the ingredients over and over to thoroughly mix, and at the same time incorporating air into the mixture. With each beating motion the spoon is brought constantly in contact with the bottom of the dish, bringing the contents over the top folding them in again. Beating is used in combination with stirring.

CUTTING and FOLDING is introducing one ingredient into a mixture, one or the other being the lighter of the two. This is accomplished with the wooden cake spoon, by making vertical cuts downward and turning mixture over, allowing the bowl of the spoon to bring the contents of the bottom of the dish over the top then folding them in again. The spoon turns entirely around in one's hand in making this motion. Repeat this motion alternately with beating until mixtures are thoroughly blended. When stiffly beaten whites of eggs are called for in a recipe they should always be cut and folded into such mixtures.

**IMPORTANT**—The foregoing instructions must be carefully followed; the ingredients called for in the recipes must be used, to insure success in the finished product. Each recipe in this Corn Cook Book has been carefully tested by an expert—a graduated teacher in household economics.

# CHAPTER I.

## HASTY PUDDING
### (Corn Meal Mush)

Put one quart of boiling water in top of the double boiler, add one and one-half teaspoons salt, mix two cups yellow or white corn meal, with two cups of cold milk, stir this slowly into the boiling water, boil five minutes, stirring constantly, then place vessel over hot water, let cook five hours stirring occasionally to prevent mush from lumping. The longer it steams the more delicious the flavor, serve with milk or cream. If white and yellow corn meal is made into "Hasty Pudding" in separate vessels, then packed in alternate layers in a brick-shaped mold, sliced when cold and served with cream and sugar, it makes a very attractive and inexpensive dessert for children.

## FRIED CORN MEAL MUSH

Prepare the mush as in the recipe above, then pack solidly into an agate brick-shape bread pan measuring seven inches long, three and one-half inches wide and two and one-half inches deep, rinsed inside with cold water so that the mush will be more easily removed when cold. Chill the mush, then turn on the cutting board and cut in slices three-quarters of an inch thick. Fry a golden brown on one side, then with a griddle cake "spade" turn and brown the other. Use lard or pure, sweet drippings. Never butter, for it burns quickly and before the mush is browned, spoiling both the look and taste of the mush. Serve with crisp bacon.

SKIMMED MILK AND BUTTER SUBSTITUTE MAY BE USED IN ALL RECIPES EXCEPT THOSE CALLING FOR CREAM.

# FRIED MUSH FAIRMONT STYLE

Pack corn meal mush into a brick-shaped bread pan (dimensions 9x4x3½ inches).  When cold, turn on a board and cut in slices one inch in thickness; dip in egg slightly beaten and diluted with two tablespoons milk, then in fine sifted cracker crumbs.  Repeat to insure their being well crumbed.  Fry to a golden brown in deep hot fat.  Drain on soft, brown paper and serve at once.

## CORN MEAL MUSH WITH LEMON FLAVOR

| | |
|---|---|
| 1 cup milk | ½ teaspoon salt |
| 1 ½ cups cold water | 4 tablespoons powdered sugar |
| ¾ cup corn meal | Thin yellow rind ½ lemon |
| 1 tablespoon butter | |

PROCESS:  Mix corn meal, salt and sugar, add milk slowly, stirring constantly, add water and lemon rind, stir until smooth and without lumps.  Place on range, bring to boiling point, continue stirring and cook five minutes.  Then cook two hours over hot water, stir occasionally.  Just before serving add butter.  Serve as a cereal with rich cream or as a dessert.  Orange rind may be used in place of lemon rind; the flavor of either is delightful.

# PAUNHAUS

1 quart boiling water  
1 quart cold water  
2 cups corn meal  
1 cup buckwheat flour  

2½ teaspoons salt  
½ teaspoon black pepper  
¼ teaspoon poultry seasoning  
½ pound liver sausage cut in small pieces  

PROCESS: Mix the dry ingredients in a bowl; moisten with the cold water, then add slowly into boiling water stirring constantly; add sausage and mix thoroughly. Cook in a cast aluminum kettle over a slow fire two and one-half hours, stirring occasionally. An asbestos mat placed under the kettle will protect mixture from scorching on bottom of kettle. Pour into agate bread pans previously wet with cold water. When cold remove from pans and cut one-half inch slices and cook as Fried Mush. Serve as the meat course at breakfast or luncheon.

## STEAMED PEARL HOMINY
### (Samp)

Soak one cup pearl hominy over night in warm water to cover. In the morning add two quarts boiling water, season with salt and heat to boiling point. Boil briskly five minutes. Reduce the heat and simmer five or six hours or until hominy is tender. Add one-fourth cup butter and serve with top milk or cream. Great care must be taken that hominy does not scorch; it should be stirred constantly the first five minutes, afterwards occasionally. If cooked in a double boiler it should steam all day, or all night in a fireless cooker.

# STEAMED SAMP

½ cup samp
Cold water
¾ teaspoon salt

1¼ cups boiling water
1¼ cups hot milk

PROCESS: Cover samp with cold water; let stand over night. Drain, put into double boiler, add boiling water, hot milk and salt. Bring to boiling point, place in lower part of double boiler containing boiling water and steam five or six hours, or cook in fireless cooker over night. Serve with top milk or cream and sugar.

# CORN MEAL DODGERS NO. 1

2 cups fine white corn meal
1 tablespoon sugar
2 eggs
1 tablespoon butter or lard

½ teaspoon salt
3 tablespoons rich milk or cream
Boiling water

PROCESS: Mix and sift corn meal, salt and sugar; add sufficient boiling water to thoroughly moisten the meal, but not to make it soft; add butter and milk; when cold add the yolks beaten very light; then cut and fold in the whites beaten until stiff. The batter should drop readily from the spoon, but not thin enough to pour nor stiff enough to be scraped from the bowl. Shape in oval cakes, lay in a hissing hot, well greased dripping pan, and bake in a very hot oven until brown and puffed; split, butter and serve with fried salt pork in cream sauce.

# CORN DODGERS NO. 2

1 quart corn meal
2 tablespoons maple or brown
  sugar

1 teaspoon salt
2 tablespoons lard
Scalded milk and water

PROCESS: Add salt, sugar and lard to corn meal; mix well, and pour over enough boiling water to make a batter to drop from tip of spoon; they should be an inch thick in the center and flatten slightly into oval cakes. Beat the batter five minutes before dropping them into a hot, well greased dripping pan. The maple sugar or syrup improves the flavor and makes the dodgers brown more richly.

# PONE CORN BREAD

2 cups corn meal (hand ground)
½ teaspoon salt
1 ¼ cups buttermilk

½ teaspoon soda
½ tablespoon melted lard,
bacon or ham fat

PROCESS: Mix well corn meal, salt and soda. Add melted fat and buttermilk, stir until well blended, then drop in oval cakes about three inches long by two and one-half inches wide on a well greased tin sheet or an inverted dripping pan. Bake twenty-five minutes in a hot oven. If not brown on top reduce heat and brown under the gas flame in broiling oven. This requires but a minute or two. Split lengthwise, butter or lay a thin slice between while piping hot and serve at once.

# CORN PONE

To one quart of white corn meal (southern milled) add one and one-half teaspoons salt, one tablespoon melted lard, and sufficient scalded milk and boiling water (equal parts) to make a mixture that can be molded with the hands into oblong cakes six inches long, three inches wide and one inch thick; they should be thin on the edges with tapering ends. Before molding them the mixture should be worked well with the hands, then shape the pones, place them on a hot, well greased tin sheet, brush over with melted butter or milk and bake twenty-five minutes in a hot oven. When done, split each one, butter and lay a thin slice of crisp bacon in each, sandwich fashion. Serve immediately.

# INDIAN BANNOCKS

1 cup corn meal 2 cups scalded milk
1 teaspoon maple syrup or sugar 2 eggs
1 teaspoon salt

PROCESS: Add corn meal gradually to scalded milk while stirring constantly, add syrup and salt; cool and add yolks beaten very lightly, then the whites beaten until stiff. Bake in a well greased, shallow pudding dish in very hot oven, twenty-five minutes. Serve in pudding dish.

# INDIAN MEAL FLAPJACKS

2 cups yellow corn meal  1 tablespoon sugar
½ teaspoon salt    Scalded milk
2 eggs       Cold milk
1 tablespoon butter

PROCESS: Mix and sift corn meal, salt and sugar, add sufficient scalded milk to moisten meal, add butter, when cool add eggs beaten until thick and lemon tinted and cold milk enough to make a thin batter. Cook on well greased, hissing hot griddle as griddle cakes.

# RHODE ISLAND JOHNNY CAKES

1 cup white corn meal  1½ teaspoons salt
1 teaspoon sugar    1 tablespoon butter
Boiling water     Cold milk

PROCESS: Pour over all boiling water enough to scald, beating constantly until a rather stiff mush is formed. Add cold milk until of the consistency to drop from tip of spoon. Drop with a spoon on a well greased, hot griddle. Cook slowly until richly browned on one side; turn and brown the other side. Serve with butter and maple syrup.

# CORN MEAL CRISPYS

1 cup corn meal   3 tablespoons melted butter
1 cup boiling water  ½ teaspoon salt

PROCESS: Sift corn meal slowly into boiling water while stirring constantly. When perfectly smooth add butter and salt. Spread smoothly on a buttered, inverted dripping pan to about one-eighth inch thickness, using a spatula. Bake in a moderate oven until richly browned. Cut in strips the size of Saratoga wafers. Remove from pan and serve immediately.

SKIMMED MILK AND BUTTER SUBSTITUTE MAY BE USED IN ALL RECIPES EXCEPT THOSE CALLING FOR CREAM.

# POLENTA WITH MUSHROOM SAUCE

| | |
|---|---|
| 2 cups boiling water | 1 teaspoon salt |
| 1 cup corn meal | ½ cup grated cheese |
| 2 cups cold water | 2 tablespoons butter |

PROCESS: Mix corn meal with cold water and gradually stir into boiling water, add salt and stir constantly until mush is smooth. Bring to boiling point and cook slowly over hot water until thoroughly cooked (about three hours). Remove from range, add butter and cheese; return to range and stir until cheese is melted and thoroughly blended with mush. Serve hot in place of meat with mushroom sauce or tomato sauce.

# MUSHROOM SAUCE

| | |
|---|---|
| 6 fresh mushrooms or ½ cup dried mushrooms | 1 small clove garlic finely chopped |
| 1 small onion finely chopped | ½ cup bacon fat or butter |
| Beef extract | ½ cup Brown Stock |

PROCESS: If fresh mushrooms are used they should be thinly sliced. If dried mushrooms are used, soak them in cold water to cover several hours or over night. Drain and reserve one-half cup of the water; finely chop mushrooms. Cook mushrooms, onion and garlic in fat until delicately browned. Heat mushroom liquor to boiling point, add beef extract stir until melted then add to mushroom mixture. Simmer ten minutes and serve in a sauce boat. The sauce may be strained if desired.

## POLENTA WITH CHEESE

2 cups boiling water  
2 cups hot milk  
1 teaspoon salt  
1 cup fine hominy  

1 cup grated cheese  
1 tablespoon Worcestershire Sauce  
Few grains cayenne  

PROCESS: Put water and milk in top vessel of double boiler, add salt and bring to boiling point; then sift in hominy very slowly while stirring constantly. Boil three minutes, continue stirring. Cook over hot water three hours or over night in a fireless cooker. Remove from range, add cheese, Worcestershire Sauce and cayenne; stir until cheese is melted; then turn into a shallow granite pan (first rinsed with cold water) to the depth of one inch. When cold cut in two and one-half-inch squares, roll carefully in fine crumbs, then in egg and again in crumbs. Fry in deep hot fat or saute in hot salt pork fat. Serve with Tomato Sauce. This dish is a splendid substitute for meat.

## SPANISH POLENTA

4 cups boiling water  
1¼ teaspoons salt  
1 medium size onion  
1 small clove garlic  

1 medium sized green pepper  
1¼ cups corn meal  
1 cup finely chopped cheese  
Few grains cayenne  

PROCESS: Pour water into top vessel of double boiler, add salt, onion, garlic and green pepper (discarding seeds and veins of latter) finely chopped; heat to boiling point then sift in corn meal slowly while stirring constantly. Add cayenne, cover and cook over boiling water two hours. Add cheese and continue cooking until cheese is melted. Serve as the main dish for luncheon or supper. May be served for dinner to help out a shortage of meat. Pass tomato sauce in a sauce boat.

# ONION CORN PONE

| | |
|---|---|
| 2 cups corn bread crumbs | ½ teaspoon salt |
| 3 tablespoons onion finely chopped | ¼ teaspoon black pepper |
| 1 tablespoon bacon fat | ¼ teaspoon Poultry Seasoning |
| 3 tablespoons hot water | 2 eggs well beaten |

PROCESS: Finely crumble cold corn bread. Measure crumbs. Melt bacon fat in an omelet pan and saute onion in fat until soft without browning. Add onion to prepared crumbs, rinse pan with hot water and add water to mixture. Sift in seasonings and add eggs beaten until thick and lemon tinted. Mix thoroughly and with the hands shape in pone cakes and cook as griddle cakes in plenty of hot salt pork fat. Serve with Brown Sauce or Tomato Sauce.

## PHILADELPHIA SCRAPPLE
### (The Real Scrapple)

Clean and cook a pig's head in boiling water to cover, until the meat slips from the bones. Remove bones and meat; finely chop meat. Strain liquor and let stand until cold, then remove fat and heat liquor to the boiling point. Add prepared meat and season highly with salt and pepper. Then sift in with one hand, while stirring with the other, enough corn meal to make mixture the consistency of mush. Let boil three or four minutes while stirring constantly, then reduce the heat and let cook slowly for two hours or more, stirring occasionally. When sufficiently cooked turn into brick-shaped agate pans and keep in a cold place. Cut in slices three-fourths of an inch thick and saute in bacon fat or salt pork fat. The scrapple will keep some time in cold weather. In some parts of Pennsylvania the scrapple is seasoned with a little sage.

**SKIMMED MILK AND BUTTER SUBSTITUTE MAY BE USED IN ALL RECIPES EXCEPT THOSE CALLING FOR CREAM.**

# SCRAPPLE WITH LIVER SAUSAGE

3 ½ cups boiling water      1 cup corn meal
1 teaspoon salt      ½ pound liver sausage

PROCESS: Add salt to boiling water, then sift corn meal through the fingers with one hand while stirring vigorously with the other. Stir until mush is smooth. Cook in a double boiler two or three hours. Remove casing from sausage, cut sausage in half-inch cubes. Add to mush, mix well and turn into a brick-shaped bread pan and chill. Cut in one-half-inch slices and saute in bacon fat or salt pork fat. Serve for breakfast.

# CHAPTER II.

## CORN MEAL MUFFINS No. 1

¼ cup yellow corn meal  
½ cup flour  
1 ½ teaspoons baking powder  
½ tablespoon sugar  
¼ teaspoon salt  
¾ tablespoon melted butter  
⅔ cup milk  
1 egg

PROCESS: Sift together the first five ingredients. Add melted butter and gradually the milk, stirring constantly. Then add egg beaten until thick and lemon tinted. Beat batter one minute. Then turn into warm, buttered iron gem pans and bake twenty-five minutes in a hot oven. Serve while hot.

## CORN MEAL MUFFINS No. 2

¼ cup butter  
¼ cup sugar  
Yolks 2 eggs well beaten  
¾ cup corn meal  
Whites 2 eggs beaten until stiff  
1 cup flour  
¾ teaspoon salt  
4 teaspoons baking powder  
1 ¼ cups sweet milk

PROCESS: Cream butter, add sugar gradually to beaten yolks. Sift together corn meal, flour, salt and baking powder; add to first mixture alternately with milk. Then fold in the beaten whites of eggs. Bake in hot, buttered iron gem cups twenty-five minutes in a hot oven.

# CORN MEAL MUFFINS WITH RICE

⅜ cup scalded milk
½ cup corn meal
⅛ cup hot cooked rice
⅛ cup flour
1 teaspoon salt

2 tablespoons sugar
3 teaspoons baking powder
1 tablespoon melted butter
1 egg

PROCESS: Pour scalded milk on corn meal, let stand five minutes. Add hot rice and mix thoroughly with the tips of fingers, add flour sifted with salt, baking powder and sugar, add melted butter, the yolk of egg beaten very light; lastly cut and fold in the white of egg beaten until stiff. Bake in well buttered, hot iron gem cups twenty minutes in hot oven.

# CURRANT MUFFINS

½ cup shortening
¾ cup sugar
3 eggs
1½ cups milk
⅓ cup dried currants or sultana raisins

2 cups corn meal
1 cup white flour
1 teaspoon salt
1½ tablespoons baking powder

PROCESS: Cream shortening; add sugar gradually, stirring constantly. Beat eggs until thick and lemon tinted, add to first mixture, continue stirring. Add milk alternately with the dry ingredients which have been sifted together. Add currants or sultana raisins slightly floured. If sultanas are large cut them in halves. Bake in well buttered gem cups twenty-five minutes in a hot oven. Serve at luncheon or supper in place of cake. These muffins are delicious and will take the place of small cakes during "War Times." The habit will then be formed and the true economist will continue their use for this purpose forever after.

SKIMMED MILK AND BUTTER SUBSTITUTE MAY BE USED IN ALL RECIPES EXCEPT THOSE CALLING FOR CREAM.

# CORN MEAL AND RICE MUFFINS

1 cup boiled rice  
⅔ cup scalded milk  
2 tablespoons strained bacon fat  
⅔ cup corn meal  
1 egg well beaten  
⅔ cup flour  
¾ teaspoon salt  
2 tablespoons sugar  
3 teaspoons baking powder

PROCESS: Add milk to rice and stir with a fork until kernels are separated; add dry ingredients sifted together, add bacon fat and beat until thoroughly blended then add egg beaten until thick and lemon tinted. Turn into well buttered, hot iron gem cups to two-thirds their depth. Bake twenty minutes in a hot oven.

# CREAM CORN MEAL GEMS

½ cup corn meal  
1 cup flour  
3 teaspoons baking powder  
2 tablespoons sugar  
½ teaspoon salt  
¾ cup cream  
1 egg lightly beaten

PROCESS: Mix and sift the dry ingredients; add cream gradually, the egg, beat well; bake in buttered gem cups twenty-five minutes in a hot oven. If a plainer gem is desired, use milk in place of cream and add one tablespoon melted butter.

# CREAM CORN MUFFINS

¾ cup corn meal  
1 cup white flour  
4 teaspoons baking powder  
¼ cup sugar  
¾ teaspoon salt  
1 cup thin cream  
2 eggs beaten very light  
4 tablespoons melted butter

PROCESS: Sift together corn meal, flour, baking powder, sugar and salt. Add cream gradually and stir to a smooth batter. Add well beaten eggs and melted butter. Beat thoroughly and bake in hissing hot, buttered gem cups in a hot oven, twenty minutes.

SKIMMED MILK AND BUTTER SUBSTITUTE MAY BE USED IN ALL RECIPES EXCEPT THOSE CALLING FOR CREAM.

# DAINTY CORN MEAL MUFFINS

½ cup corn meal  
½ cup boiling water  
2 tablespoons butter  
¼ cup pastry flour  
⅛ teaspoon salt  

Few grains mace  
2 teaspoons baking powder  
3 tablespoons sugar  
1 egg well beaten  
½ cup top milk  

PROCESS: Pour boiling water over corn meal, add butter and stir until well mixed. Cover and let stand an hour or two. Add flour sifted with salt, mace, baking powder and sugar. Add milk and well beaten egg, beating constantly. Bake in well buttered, small muffin pans twenty minutes. This recipe makes twelve small muffins.

# RICH CORN MEAL MUFFINS

¼ cup butter  
¼ cup sugar  
Yolks 2 eggs well beaten  
¾ cup corn meal  
Whites 2 eggs beaten until stiff  

1 cup flour  
¾ teaspoon salt  
4 teaspoons baking powder  
1 ¼ cups sweet milk  

PROCESS: Cream butter, add sugar gradually to well beaten yolks. Sift together corn meal, flour, salt and baking powder; add to first mixture alternately with milk, then fold in the beaten whites of eggs. Bake in hot, buttered iron gem cups twenty-five minutes in a hot oven.

## CORN MEAL AND BARLEY MEAL MUFFINS

¾ cup corn meal
½ cup barley meal
1 cup flour
3 tablespoons baking powder
½ teaspoon salt

¼ teaspoon soda
⅓ cup molasses
1 egg and 1 egg yolk
1 cup thick sour milk
3 tablespoons sausage fat

PROCESS: Sift together the dry ingredients; add molasses and well beaten eggs; then gradually pour in sour milk while stirring constantly; add melted shortening and if mixture appears too thick add more sour milk. Bake in hot well greased iron muffin cups in a hot oven, twenty-five minutes. If these muffins are made with sweet milk the soda must be omitted. Serve hot.

## CORN MEAL POPOVERS

2 cups scalded milk
1 cup corn meal
1 tablespoon butter

½ teaspoon salt
3 eggs beaten very light

PROCESS: Stir corn meal into hot milk; add butter and salt, cool slightly and add eggs, beat mixture two minutes and turn into hissing hot, well greased iron gem cups; bake thirty-five minutes in a hot oven; strongest heat must come from bottom.

## CORN MEAL FOR CRUMBING FISH

For crumbing fish for sauteing or frying; use seasoned corn meal. Season the meal to be used for this purpose with salt and pepper; roll the fish in the meal, dip in egg and again roll in meal. Then saute fish in salt pork fat or fry in deep, hot fat.

# PARKER HOUSE CORN ROLLS

| | |
|---|---|
| 1 ⅛ cup white flour | 1 tablespoon sugar |
| ¾ cup corn meal | 2 tablespoons butter |
| 4 teaspoons baking powder | 1 egg |
| ½ teaspoon salt | ½ cup milk |

PROCESS: Sift together dry ingredients; rub in butter with the tips of fingers; beat egg until thick and lemon tinted, add one-half cupmilk, add to first mixture, add remaining milk if necessary. The dough must be soft as can be handled. Turn on a floured board, knead slightly and roll to one-half-inch thickness. Shape with a small biscuit cutter, crease through center of each round with handle of knife, brush one-half of each round with soft butter; fold as Parker House rolls, press edges lightly together. Arrange on a buttered baking sheet and bake fifteen minutes in a hot oven. Serve at once.

# HOMINY AND CORN MEAL MUFFINS

| | |
|---|---|
| ¼ cup fine hominy | ½ cup corn meal |
| 1 teaspoon salt | 4 tablespoons sugar |
| 2 tablespoons butter | Yolks 2 eggs |
| ½ cup boiling water | 4 teaspoons baking powder |
| 1 cup scalded milk | Whites 2 eggs |

PROCESS: Cook hominy, salt and butter in double boiler twenty-five minutes, cool. Pour scalded milk over corn meal, add sugar and hominy; yolks of eggs beaten until thick and light. Sift in baking powder and fold in the whites of eggs beaten until stiff. Bake in hot iron gem cups well buttered thirty minutes.

# HOMINY MUFFINS

1 cup hominy porridge packed solidly  
2 cups flour  
2 teaspoons sugar  
4 teaspoons baking powder  
¾ teaspoon salt  
⅔ cup milk  
2 tablespoons melted butter  
2 eggs beaten very light

PROCESS: Sift together flour, salt, sugar and baking powder, add porridge and mix well, add melted butter and milk, beat until free from lumps. Add eggs beaten until thick and lemon tinted. Bake twenty-five minutes in a hot oven, in hot, well buttered iron gem cups.

# POPPETS

1 cup corn meal  
1 cup flour  
1 tablespoon sugar  
1 teaspoon salt  
1 tablespoon melted butter  
4 teaspoons baking powder  
2 cups rich milk  
1 egg

PROCESS: Mix and sift the dry ingredients, add butter, egg, beaten until thick and lemon tinted and added to milk; stir into first mixture and beat batter three minutes. Pour into hissing hot, well greased gem cups and bake in hot oven thirty minutes.

# CORN STICKS

1 cup corn meal  
¾ cup flour  
3 teaspoons baking powder  
½ teaspoon salt  
½ cup hot boiled pearl hominy  
¼ cup butter  
1 cup milk  
2 eggs well beaten

PROCESS: To hot hominy add butter, milk and well beaten eggs; add to dry ingredients that have been sifted together. Beat thoroughly and turn into buttered bread-stick pans and bake in a moderate oven, twenty-five minutes.

**SKIMMED MILK AND BUTTER SUBSTITUTE MAY BE USED IN ALL RECIPES EXCEPT THOSE CALLING FOR CREAM.**

# CORN MEAL YORKSHIRE PUDDING

Pour one cup of boiling water over one cup of white corn meal, while stirring constantly; add one-half teaspoon salt and two eggs beaten until thick and lemon-tinted. Pour some of the dripping from the roasting meat into a shallow baking dish, turn in the mixture, spread evenly and bake in an oven thirty-five minutes; baste three times while baking with some of the dripping from roasting pan. Serve hot, cut in squares, with roast beef, lamb or pork.

# CORN MEAL GRIDDLE CAKES NO. 2
## (Small Recipe)

| | |
|---|---|
| 1 cup corn meal (Burr milled) | 1 cup thick sour milk |
| ¼ cup flour | ¼ teaspoon soda |
| ¼ teaspoon salt | 1 egg |
| 2 teaspoons baking powder | 2 tablespoons melted bacon, sausage fat or butter |

PROCESS: Sift flour, salt and baking powder into corn meal, mix well. Dissolve soda in the sour milk and add gradually to dry ingredients, stirring constantly. Add egg beaten until thick and lemon tinted and melted fat, beat mixture two minutes. Cook as griddle cakes. This recipe makes ten medium sized griddle cakes.

# SOUR MILK CORN CAKES

1 cup yellow corn meal  
½ cup flour  
½ teaspoon salt  
1 tablespoon bacon or sausage fat  

1 egg well beaten  
¾ teaspoon soda  
1¼ cups rich sour milk  

PROCESS: Sift together corn meal, flour and salt. Beat egg until thick and lemon tinted, add to dry ingredients, mix well. Dissolve soda in milk and add to mixture gradually while stirring constantly. Add bacon fat and beat batter one minute. Fry at once on a well greased, hot griddle. If batter stands too long it will thicken and may then be thinned by adding more sour milk. Cook as other griddle cakes.

## CORN MEAL AND RICE GRIDDLE CAKES
### (Sour Milk)

1 cup corn meal  
⅜ cup flour  
1 teaspoon salt  
1 teaspoon soda  
1 egg beaten until very light  

2 tablespoons sugar  
1 cup cooked rice  
1 cup thick sour cream or  
   country buttermilk  

PROCESS: Sift together the dry ingredients; add rice and with the fingers mix it thoroughly with the dry ingredients, add sour milk or cream gradually, stirring constantly, then the well beaten egg. Beat batter two minutes and cook as other griddle cakes.

## CORN MEAL AND RICE GRIDDLE CAKES
### (With Sweet Milk)

| | |
|---|---|
| 1 cup corn meal | 1 cup sweet milk |
| 2 cups cold boiled rice | 1 tablespoon molasses |
| ½ cup flour | 1 tablespoon melted sausage |
| 4 teaspoons baking powder |   fat or butter |
| 1 ¼ teaspoons salt | 2 well beaten eggs |

PROCESS: Add corn meal to rice and mix thoroughly with the hand. Sift together flour, baking powder and salt. Add to first mixture alternately with milk, stirring constantly. Add molasses and shortening, continue stirring, then fold in the lightly beaten eggs. Beat mixture two minutes and cook as griddle cakes. Serve with lemon, orange or maple syrup.

## "DELICIA" CORN MEAL AND BROWN RICE
## GRIDDLE CAKES

| | |
|---|---|
| 1 cup corn meal | ½ teaspoon salt |
| 1 cup cooked brown rice | 1 teaspoon soda |
| ½ cup flour | 1 ¼ cups rich sour milk |
| | 2 eggs well beaten |

PROCESS: Sift together the dry ingredients; add rice and mix thoroughly; add sour milk gradually, stirring constantly. Add eggs and beat mixture two minutes. Cook as other griddle cakes. If the milk is not rich, add two tablespoons bacon or sausage fat.

# CORN MEAL GRIDDLE CAKES NO. 1
## (With Milk and Water)

1½ cups corn meal
½ cup flour
4 teaspoons baking powder
1 teaspoon salt
1 egg

1 tablespoon Karo syrup
1 tablespoon bacon or sausage
   fat
½ cup milk
¾ cup cold water

PROCESS: Sift together flour, baking powder and salt. Add corn meal, stir thoroughly, add syrup, melted fat and milk, stirring constantly; add water and egg beaten until thick and lemon tinted. Beat mixture two minutes and cook as other griddle cakes immediately. If this batter is allowed to stand too long before using it may be necessary to add more baking powder to replace that which has been lost by long standing.

# SCALDED CORN MEAL GRIDDLE CAKES
## (Old Alabama Recipe)

2 cups corn meal
1½ cups boiling water
1 teaspoon salt

Yolks 3 eggs
½ cup milk
Whites 3 eggs

PROCESS: Pour boiling water over corn meal mixed with salt; stir until well mixed and moistened throughout. Beat egg yolks until thick and light, add to first mixture, stirring constantly, add milk gradually and continue stirring. Beat whites of eggs until stiff, then cut and fold them carefully into batter. Beat two minutes. Cook as griddle cakes. Serve with crips bacon.

## "PETE'S" CORN MEAL GRIDDLE CAKES

2 cups corn meal
1 cup flour
2 eggs well beaten
1 teaspoon salt

1 ½ teaspoons soda
2 ½ cups buttermilk or
   clappered milk

PROCESS: Mix and sift corn meal, flour and salt; add eggs, mix well. Dissolve soda in milk; add to first mixture. Beat thoroughly and fry at once. If allowed to stand too long mixture thickens; may be thinned by adding more milk. The sour milk must be rich. Buttermilk is best for this purpose.

## CORN MEAL AND BUCKWHEAT GRIDDLE CAKES

½ cup corn meal (hand ground)
¾ cup buckwheat flour
⅓ cup bread flour
½ teaspoon salt
1 teaspoon sugar
1 egg well beaten

1 teaspoon soda dissolved in
   1 ¼ cups buttermilk
½ tablespoon melted butter
   or sausage fat
1 tablespoon molasses

PROCESS: Sift buckwheat, flour, salt and sugar into corn meal, (do not sift the latter), add one cup buttermilk, melted butter and soda dissolved in remaining one-fourth cup buttermilk, stirring constantly; add molasses and well beaten egg. Beat batter two minutes and cook as other griddle cakes.

## LEFT OVER GRANULATED HOMINY GRIDDLE CAKES

1 cup cold cooked granulated
  hominy
1 well beaten egg
1 cup milk
1 cup flour

2 ½ teaspoons baking powder
1 tablespoon sugar
¾ teaspoon salt
⅛ teaspoon nutmeg or mace
1 tablespoon melted butter

PROCESS: Put hominy into mixing bowl, add egg beaten until thick and lemon tinted, stir constantly while adding milk gradually. Sift together flour, baking powder, salt, sugar and nutmeg, add gradually to first mixture, beating and stirring until all ingredients are well blended. Add melted butter, stir two minutes and cook as griddle cakes. Serve with brown sugar syrup.

## FLANNEL CAKES NO. 1

2 cups scalded milk
½ compressed yeast-cake
⅛ cup corn meal
1 cup white flour

½ teaspoon salt
1 tablespoon melted butter
1 egg

PROCESS: Set the following mixture to rise over night; scald meal with milk, add butter and flour; when mixture is lukewarm add yeast dissolved in one-fourth cup of lukewarm water; cover and set to rise in a warm place (68 degrees F.). In the morning add salt and egg; yolk and white beaten separately. Cook as griddle cakes.

# FLANNEL CAKES NO. 2

1 ½ cups corn meal  
3 cups scalded milk  
¼ cup strained bacon or sausage fat  
½ tablespoon salt  
2 tablespoons molasses or sugar  
½ yeast-cake dissolved in  
¼ cup lukewarm water  
1 ½ cups flour or rye meal

PROCESS: Pour scalded milk over corn meal; add fat and when lukewarm add remaining ingredients. Cover and set to rise in a warm place over night. In the morning beat mixture lightly and cook as griddle cakes.

# HOMINY WAFFLES NO. 1

1 cup cooked granulated hominy packed solidly  
½ cup corn meal  
2 cups flour  
1 teaspoon salt  
1 ½ tablespoons baking powder  
1 cup rich milk  
¼ cup melted butter or bacon fat  
3 eggs

PROCESS: Sift together corn meal, flour, salt and baking powder, add hominy and mix thoroughly until mixture is like meal. Add milk gradually, stirring constantly, then add melted fat and eggs beaten until thick and lemon tinted. Beat mixture until smooth and well blended. Cook in a hot, well greased waffle iron. This recipe will make eight large waffles. Serve with lemon or orange syrup.

# HOMINY GRIDDLE CAKES

1 cup cooked hominy  
2 cups flour  
5 teaspoons baking powder  
1 egg  
¾ teaspoon salt  
1 cup sweet milk  
3 tablespoons cream  

PROCESS: Sift together flour, baking powder and salt; add cold porridge and mix thoroughly to prevent mixture from being lumpy; beat egg until thick and lemon tinted; add milk and cream to egg and combine with first mixture; beat thoroughly and fry as girddle cakes.

# HOMINY WAFFLES NO. 2

1 cup hominy porridge packed solidly  
2½ cups flour  
1 cup milk  
3 tablespoons melted butter  
5 teaspoons baking powder  
¾ teaspoon salt  
3 eggs beaten thick and light  

PROCESS: Sift together flour, salt and baking powder; add porridge, mix thoroughly, add butter; pour milk into beaten eggs and add to first mixture; beat until free from lumps; fry in hot, well greased waffle iron, allowing three cook's spoons to each waffle. If mixture appears too thick, add more milk.

# NORFOLK WAFFLES

1½ cups boiling water  
½ cup corn meal  
1½ cups milk  
3 cups flour  
3 tablespoons sugar  
3½ teaspoons baking powder  
1½ teaspoons salt  
3 eggs  
2 tablespoons butter  

PROCESS: Cook corn meal in water twenty minutes; add milk and dry ingredients sifted together. When slightly cooled add yolks of eggs lightly beaten, butter and whites of eggs beaten until stiff. Cook in hot, well greased waffle iron. Serve immediately.

# GRANULATED HOMINY CRUSTS

1 cup boiled granulated hominy    1 egg
2 tablespoons sugar    Flour, salt and milk

PROCESS: Cook the hominy in double boiler, in milk enough to make a thin batter and until the hominy is very soft. Add salt to taste and when lukewarm egg well beaten and sufficient flour to hold mixture together. Spread in well buttered, shallow pan to one-third inch thickness. Bake in hot oven. Split and serve with butter and maple syrup.

## SAVORY HOMINY
### Serve with Roast Goose, Ducks and Pork

To two cups of hot steamed or boiled hominy well seasoned with salt add one-third cup of butter or butterine, one-fourth cup finely chopped white onions and one and one-half tablespoons finely chopped parsley. Mix thoroughly. If too dry moisten with a little hot condensed milk or cream. Serve in place of potatoes with roast goose, ducks or pork. This mixture may be used for stuffing goose or domestic ducks.

## HOMINY CROQUETTES

Shape into balls one quart of well cooked, highly seasoned granulated hominy. Roll in cracker crumbs, dip in egg, slightly beaten and diluted with two tablespoons cold water, then again in cracker crumbs. Fry in deep fat. Drain on brown paper and serve as a vegetable with Cheese Sauce; or sweeten the mixture to taste, flavor with grated lemon peel, shape, crumb and fry; serve as dessert with maple syrup.

SKIMMED MILK AND BUTTER SUBSTITUTE MAY BE USED IN ALL
RECIPES EXCEPT THOSE CALLING FOR CREAM.

# HOMINY AND HORSE-RADISH CROQUETTES

¼ cup granulated hominy  
½ cup boiling water  
½ teaspoon salt  
¾ cup scalded milk  

2 tablespoons butter or butter substitute  
3½ tablespoons grated horse-radish  
1 tablespoon grated onion or chopped chives  

PROCESS: Cook hominy with water in a double boiler until water is absorbed; add salt and milk and continue cooking until hominy is soft. Add butter, horse-radish and onion. Spread mixture on a plate. When cool, shape in balls, roll in crumbs, egg and crumbs and fry in deep, hot fat. Drain on brown paper and serve with roast pork, baked ham, pork tenderloin, etc.

## HOMINY BALLS
### (Serve as a Vegetable)

1 quart boiled granulated hominy  
½ cup grated cheese  
Egg and crumbs  

½ tablespoon grated onion  
1 teaspoon finely chopped parsley  

PROCESS: Add cheese, onion and parsley to hot, well seasoned hominy, cool and shape into balls the size of a small lemon, roll in fine crumbs, egg and crumbs and fry in deep hot fat. Drain on soft, brown paper and serve with roast pork, lamb, etc.

# HOMINY WITH TOMATOES

2 cups canned hulled corn or
  cooked pearl hominy
1 cup thick tomato pulp
2 tablespoons bacon fat or butter

2 tablespoons flour
½ teaspoon salt
⅛ teaspoon pepper
Fine buttered cracker crumbs

PROCESS:  Melt fat in a sauce-pan, add flour and stir until well blended; add strained tomato pulp, salt and pepper.  Add hulled corn mixed well and turn into a buttered baking dish.  Cover with prepared cracker crumbs and bake thirty minutes in a hot oven.  One teaspoon of onion juice may be added to the tomato mixture before combining with corn.  Serve in place of potatoes.

# PEARL HOMINY WITH MINCED HAM

2 cups boiled or steamed hominy
½ cup finely minced left-over
  ham
2 tablespoons ham fat
1 ½ tablespoons flour

1 cup skimmed milk
½ teaspoon salt
⅛ teaspoon pepper
½ tablespoon finely chopped
  parsley
Paprika

PROCESS:  Cook pearl hominy as directed on Page 13.  Measure the left-over hominy and mix thoroughly with minced ham.  Prepare a white sauce with remaining ingredients (except paprika).  Add hominy mixture, place on range and bring to boiling point; stir until heated through; then turn into a warm serving dish and sprinkle with paprika.  Serve at breakfast, luncheon or supper.

## SAMP AU GRATIN

Blanch one cup of Baltimore samp in boiling water
ten minutes, drain and cover with fresh boiling water.
Heat to the boiling point and cook fifteen minutes,
stirring occasionally. Cover and place vessel on a thick
asbestos mat and continue cooking very slowly until
samp is soft; from eight to ten hours. (This may be
cooked over night in a fireless cooker.) Make a White
Sauce No. 2, adding one-fourth teaspoon paprika and
one tablespoon finely chopped chives or grated onion to
sauce. To the sauce add one and one-half cup of the
prepared samp and two-thirds cup of grated cheese.
Turn mixture into a buttered baking dish and sprinkle
top thickly with buttered and seasoned cracker crumbs.
Bake in the oven until mixture is heated throughout
and crumbs are browned. Serve as main dish at luncheon
or supper or it may supply a shortage in meat at dinner.

## HOMINY PUFF

| | |
|---|---|
| 1 cup cold boiled hominy | 2 eggs |
| 1 cup white corn meal | 1 teaspoon salt |
| 2 tablespoons butter or | 1 tablespoon baking powder |
|   butterine | 1½ cups milk |

PROCESS: Mix hominy with corn meal, then sift
in salt and baking powder. Add yolks of eggs beaten
until thick and lemon tinted and melted butter. Add
milk gradually while stirring constantly, then fold in
the stiffly beaten whites of eggs. Turn mixture into a
well greased baking dish and bake slowly for one-half
hour. Serve with roast pork, lamb or beef.

# HOMINY BOULETTES

3 cups water
1 teaspoon salt
¾ cup granulated hominy
1 teaspoon onion juice
1 tablespoon melted butter

⅛ teaspoon white pepper
½ teaspoon finely chopped
  parsley
¼ teaspoon Poultry Seasoning

PROCESS: Put water in top vessel of double boiler, bring to boiling point, season with salt and add hominy slowly so as not to stop water from boiling, stirring constantly. Cook over a low fire five minutes, continue stirring. Remove to lower part of boiler and cook over boiling water three hours or longer. Remove from range, add seasonings in the order given, mix thoroughly; spread on a plate to cool. Then with the hands shape in balls the size of an egg, roll in fine cracker crumbs, then in egg (diluted with two tablespoons cold water), again in crumbs and fry in deep, hot fat. Serve in place of potatoes.

# THIN WHITE SAUCE

2 tablespoons butter
1 ½ tablespoons flour

¼ teaspoon salt
Few grains pepper
1 cup hot milk

PROCESS: Melt the butter in a saucepan; add flour mixed with the seasonings; let cook one minute; stir to a smooth paste. Then add milk gradually and beat with gem whip until smooth and glossy.

# GNOCCHI A LA ROMAINE

3 tablespoons corn meal  
¼ cup cornstarch  
½ teaspoon salt  
¼ teaspoon paprika  
2 cups milk  

2 tablespoons butter or  
  butter substitute  
Yolks 2 eggs  
¾ cup grated cheese  
Few grains cayenne and salt  

PROCESS: Mix corn meal, corn-starch, salt and paprika. Add enough of the milk to make of a smooth consistency. Scald remaining milk in a double boiler; then stir in the first mixture slowly, beating constantly until mixture thickens. Cover and cook two hours, stirring occasionally. Remove from range. Cream butter, add egg yolks slightly beaten; add to cooked mixture and beat thoroughly. Stir in cheese and return to range and continue cooking until cheese is melted and mixture is puffed slightly. Turn into a buttered pan to the depth of one inch. Chill. Cut into squares and arrange in a shallow baking dish. Sprinkle with grated cheese, seasoned with cayenne and salt. Place in a moderate oven until heated through and cheese is melted.

## CASSEROLE OF HOMINY WITH MEAT

Finely chop cooked pearl hominy and slightly moisten with a little White Sauce. Line a quart brick-shaped mold or bread pan to the depth of one inch thickness with the prepared hominy, leaving a cavity in the center. Mince any kind of left-over meat or fowl; there should be one cup. Moisten meat with a little Brown Sauce, White Sauce or Tomato Sauce. Fill cavity with meat and cover with more hominy. Cover mold or if a bread pan is used cover with a buttered paper. Cook in a steamer thirty-five minutes. Unmold on warm serving platter and pour around Brown or Tomato Sauce.

# GNOCCHI AU GRATIN

1 ½ cups fine hominy or corn meal　1 cup grated cheese
1 cup milk　½ cup cracker crumbs
1 ½ tablespoons butter　3 tablespoons melted butter
Thin white sauce (about 1 ½ cups)　½ teaspoon salt
Few grains cayenne

PROCESS: Scald milk in double boiler, add butter and salt and sift in slowly the hominy or corn meal, stirring constantly. Cook until mixture becomes a stiff paste. Mold mixture into quennelles with two teaspoons, poach these in simmering chicken stock or boiling, salted water. Drain and arrange them in a shallow baking dish in a layer, cover with white sauce and a thin layer of grated cheese, a few grains cayenne. Continue with layers until all materials are used, having a thin layer of sauce and cheese on top. Butter the cracker crumbs and sprinkle over top. Bake in hot oven fifteen minutes. Bechamel Sauce may be used in place of white sauce, making this dish still more delicious.

# HOMINY CRUSTS

1 cup cooked fine hominy　1 egg well beaten
2 tablespoons sugar　Flour, salt and milk

PROCESS: Cook hominy in double boiler in enough milk to make a thin batter and until hominy is soft. Season with salt and when lukewarm add egg beaten until thick and lemon tinted and sufficient white flour to hold mixture together. Spread in a well greased, shallow pan to one-half inch thickness. Bake in a hot oven until brown and crisp. Split and spread with butter. Serve with maple syrup.

# BECHAMEL SAUCE

4 tablespoons butter  
4 tablespoons flour  
Salt and pepper  

1 cup highly seasoned chicken  
  stock  
1 cup hot cream  
Nutmeg  

PROCESS: Melt butter in saucepan; add flour; stir to a smooth paste. Cook one minute. Add stock, beating constantly; add cream and a slight grating of nutmeg. Beat.

# TOMATO SAUCE

4 tablespoons butter  
5½ tablespoons flour  
1½ cups brown stock  
1½ cups stewed and strained  
  tomatoes  
1 slice carrot  
1 slice onion  

Bit of bay leaf  
Sprig of parsley  
4 cloves  
¾ teaspoon salt  
¼ teaspoon pepper  
Few grains cayenne  

PROCESS: Brown butter in saucepan; add flour; stir to a smooth paste and continue browning. Add seasonings, pour on gradually, brown stock, stirring constantly. Add tomato pulp, stir briskly and let simmer fifteen minutes. Strain and serve.

# CHEESE SAUCE

| | |
|---|---|
| 2 tablespoons butter | ⅛ teaspoon white pepper |
| 1½ tablespoons flour | Few grains cayenne |
| 1 cup scalded milk | ¾ cup cheese cut in small |
| ⅛ teaspoon salt | pieces |

PROCESS: Melt butter in a saucepan; add flour mixed with seasonings. Stir to a smooth paste. Add milk gradually, stirring constantly until smooth and glossy. Add cheese when melted; pour over hot hulled corn or serve with hominy croquettes.

## SUBSTITUTES TO USE FOR "BUTTERING" CRUMBS

Prepare the crumbs in the usual way i. e., by grating, rolling as in the case of crackers or rubbing "fresh" stale bread crumbs through a wire croquette basket or passing stale bread through a meat chopper. For fine crumbs, sifting the crumbs should follow the first part of the process. To one cup of prepared crumbs, melt four tablespoons of oleomargarine, strained bacon fat or sausage fat. Add crumbs and stir until well blended. The two latter fats will impart a savory flavor to all such meat and vegetable mixtures as are made up into croquettes, also to many of the au gratin dishes. Try them.

# CHAPTER III.

## QUICK WAR BREAD

1 ½ cups stale bread crumbs  
3 ¼ cups cold water  
¾ cup molasses  
½ tablespoon salt  

2 cups corn meal  
2 ½ cups rye meal  
1 tablespoon soda  
¾ cup shredded raisins  

PROCESS: Soak bread crumbs in two cups of water over night. In the morning rub through a colander, (without draining) add molasses and dry ingredients sifted together, mix with raisins, add remaining water and beat thoroughly. Turn into well buttered, brown bread molds, filling them two-thirds full. Adjust covers and tie on securely. Steam two hours.

## BOSTON BROWN BREAD

1 cup corn meal  
1 cup rye meal  
1 cup Graham flour  
2 ½ teaspoons soda  

1 teaspoon salt  
¾ cup N. O. molasses  
2 cups sour milk or 1 ¾ cups  
of sweet milk or water  

PROCESS: Sift together the dry ingredients, add the molasses and gradually milk, beat thoroughly, turn into well buttered molds and steam three and one-half hours. The covers should be buttered before placing them on molds and tied down with a string if they do not lock. Remove covers and set molds in oven to dry off top of loaves.

## BOSTON BROWN BREAD WITH FRUIT

Follow recipe for Boston Brown Bread, adding three-fourths cup seeded and shredded raisins, add these to the dry ingredients, then continue as in foregoing recipe.

## STEAMED BROWN BREAD

2 ½ cups corn meal  
1 teaspoon salt  
¾ tablespoon soda  

2 ½ cups graham flour  
1 cup molasses  
2 ½ cups rich sour milk  

PROCESS: Sift together the first three ingredients; add unsifted graham flour. Add molasses to sour milk and stir into first mixture. Mix well and beat two minutes. Turn mixture into well buttered brown bread molds to two-thirds their depth and steam three and one-half hours. The water must continue to boil throughout the entire period of steaming. This mixture may be baked in a well buttered, small iron bread pan.

## STEAMED CORN MEAL
### (Raisin or Date Bread)

1 ½ cups corn meal  
1 cup rye meal  
½ cup flour  
1 ½ teaspoons soda  
1 cup milk  

1 teaspoon salt  
¾ cup molasses  
1 cup water  
1 cup dates stoned and cut in small pieces or seeded raisins cut in halves  

PROCESS: Sift together the dry ingredients; add dates or raisins, then add molasses, water and milk gradually while stirring constantly until well mixed. Turn into well greased, brown bread molds to two-thirds their depth and steam three hours.

SKIMMED MILK AND BUTTER SUBSTITUTE MAY BE USED IN ALL RECIPES EXCEPT THOSE CALLING FOR CREAM.

# JOLLY JOE

2 cups corn meal  
2 cups flour  
1 teaspoon salt  
1 cup N. O. molasses  

2 cups sour milk  
2 ½ teaspoons soda  
2 tablespoons hot water  

PROCESS: Sift together corn meal, flour and salt; add molasses and sour milk, beat thoroughly, then add soda dissolved in hot water. Turn into a well buttered mold, adjust cover, tie securely and steam three to four hours. Two-thirds cup of seeded and shredded raisins may be added to this mixture if fruit brown bread is liked.

## CORN MEAL DATE BREAD
### (Quick Bread)

¾ cup corn meal  
¾ cup white flour  
1 cup graham flour  
½ tablespoon salt  
1 ¾ tablespoon baking powder  
¼ teaspoon soda  
1 egg well beaten  

¼ cup molasses  
1 cup dates stoned and cut in pieces  
½ cup English walnut meats broken in pieces  
Grated rind ½ lemon  
1 tablespoon melted lard  
1 ⅛ cups skimmed milk  

PROCESS: Sift together the dry ingredients. Add the dates and walnut meats. Add molasses, shortening and milk gradually, stirring constantly. Add egg beaten until thick and lemon tinted and grated lemon rind. Beat until ingredients are well blended. Turn into a well greased, brick-shaped bread pan, cover. Let stand twenty minutes. Bake in a "bread oven" fifty minutes.

# FRIED CORN MEAL MUFFINS

1 cup corn meal  
2 cups scalded milk  
2 eggs unbeaten  

½ cup flour  
1 tablespoon sugar  
1 teaspoon salt  
1 tablespoon bacon fat

PROCESS: Pour scalded milk over corn meal; mix well and let stand until cold. Add eggs one at a time and stir thoroughly between each addition. Sift together flour, sugar and salt. Add to first mixture and beat one minute. Drop by tablespoonfuls into deep, hot fat, fry and turn as doughnuts until well browned. The fat should not be too hot when muffins are dropped in; after the first two minutes increase the heat and finish frying. Drain on brown paper; split, butter and serve at once.

# INDIAN MEAL AND RYE MEAL BREAD

4 cups corn meal  
Boiling water  
2 cups rye meal or flour  
1 tablespoon salt  

¼ cup molasses  
½ teaspoon soda  
½ yeast-cake dissolved in  
   ½ cup lukewarm water  
Warm water

PROCESS: Pour boiling water over corn meal and rye meal mixed together, to moisten but not to form a batter, stirring constantly. Add molasses, salt and soda sifted together. When mixture is lukewarm add dissolved yeast-cake and stir until well blended; then add enough lukewarm water to make a batter as stiff as can be beaten; cover; set in a warm place to rise over night. In the morning turn into a well greased, deep, agate pan; smooth the top with the hand dipped in water, cover and set to rise for half an hour. Bake in a slow oven two and one-half hours; cover the first hour of baking with a greased paper to prevent baking too hard on top before baking through. This bread was originally baked in an iron pot with a cover (what is now called a Dutch oven). It was one of the breads of our forefathers and is delicious. Try it.

## INDIAN MEAL BREAD
### (With Yeast)

1 cup corn meal
1 cup scalded milk
1 cup boiling water
2 tablespoons shortening
Rye or white flour

2 tablespoons sugar
1 tablespoon salt
⅛ yeast-cake dissolved in ½
   cup lukewarm water

PROCESS: Put corn meal into a mixing bowl, pour over scalded milk mixed with boiling water; add shortening, sugar and salt. When mixture is lukewarm add dissolved yeast-cake and flour enough to make a stiff dough (from five to six cups). Knead until smooth and elastic. Cover and set in a warm place (out of a draft) over night. In the morning turn on a floured board, knead slightly and shape into loaves, let rise. Bake one hour.

## RAISED BROWN BREAD NO. 2

2 cups boiling water
2 cups corn meal
⅛ yeast cake dissolved in ½
   cup lukewarm water

2 cups rye meal or flour
½ cup brown sugar or molasses
2 teaspoons salt
⅛ teaspoon soda

PROCESS: Pour boiling water over corn meal. When lukewarm add yeast-cake dissolved in half cup lukewarm water; add remaining ingredients in the order given. Beat thoroughly, cover closely and set in a warm place to rise over night. In the morning beat, pour into buttered bread pans and bake in a moderate oven from one and one-half to two hours. This bread is best baked in an iron brown-bread pan or a bowl-shaped crock.

**SKIMMED MILK AND BUTTER SUBSTITUTE MAY BE USED IN ALL RECIPES EXCEPT THOSE CALLING FOR CREAM.**

# CORN MEAL AND GRAHAM BREAD

1 cup corn meal  
1 cup boiling water  
1 cup scalded milk  
2 tablespoons lard  
Graham flour  

1 tablespoon salt  
¼ cup brown sugar or molasses  
½ compressed yeast cake  
⅓ cup lukewarm water  

PROCESS: Pour boiling water over corn meal; stir until well mixed, add milk and lard; when lukewarm add salt, molasses and yeast-cake, dissolved in lukewarm water. Add about four cups of graham flour, a little more may be needed, beat thoroughly, cover, set to rise in a warm place until double in bulk; stir down and beat again. Turn into well greased brick-shaped bread pans, cover and again set to rise. When light bake one hour, having the initial heat greatest for the first fifteen minutes.

# RAISED CORN MUFFINS

1 cup scalded milk  
¼ cup lard  
¼ cup sugar  
2 teaspoons salt  

¼ compressed yeast cake dissolved in ¼ cup lukewarm water  
1¼ cups corn meal  
1¼ cups flour  

PROCESS: To scalded milk add shortening, sugar and salt. When lukewarm add dissolved yeast-cake, corn meal and flour, beat vigorously and fill to half their depth, warm well greased iron gem cups. Let rise to double their bulk, then bake thirty minutes in a hot oven.

# RAISED CORN FLOUR PARKER HOUSE ROLLS

1 ⅜ cups corn flour  
2 ¼ cups scalded milk  
1 yeast cake dissolved in ½  
  cup lukewarm water  
White 1 egg

1 cup white flour  
⅛ cup shortening  
2 tablespoons sugar  
1 tablespoon salt

PROCESS: Pour scalded milk slowly over corn flour, stirring constantly, cover and let stand until lukewarm; add dissolved yeast-cake and gradually one cup white flour stirring constantly until sponge is smooth. Cover, set in a warm place until light, foamy and full of bubbles. Add remaining ingredients (except egg white). Beat vigorously then add white of egg beaten until stiff. Add sufficient white flour to handle. Knead until smooth and elastic. Cover and set to rise. When double in bulk turn on a floured board, knead slightly and roll into a sheet one-half inch in thickness; brush over lightly with melted butter, shape with biscuit cutter, make a crease across each round with the floured handle of a small wooden spoon; fold, press edges lightly and bake in a hot oven twenty-five minutes. Corn flour is finely bolted corn meal and should be used for all raised corn mixtures and sweet cakes, cookies, etc., made from corn products.

# SOUTH CAROLINA SPOON CORN BREAD

2 cups fine hominy  
6 cups boiling salted water  
2 tablespoons strained bacon fat  
3 eggs  

2 cups milk  
2 cups corn meal  
Salt  
Milk  

PROCESS: Add hominy slowly to boiling salted water until mixture thickens; then cook over boiling water until soft (about one hour). Remove from range and while hot add bacon fat, eggs beaten until thick and lemon tinted; add milk and slowly corn meal; add salt if necessary. The mixture should be the consistency of boiled custard. If too thick and dry add more milk. Turn into a well buttered baking dish and cook in the oven until mixture is firm. Serve at once in the dish in which it was baked.

# SOUTHERN CORN BREAD

1½ cups cold cooked rice or  
  granulated hominy  
2 cups milk  
1 cup corn meal  

1 teaspoon salt  
¼ cup butter  
2 eggs  

PROCESS: Scald two-thirds of the milk in a double boiler; then stir in the rice or hominy, pour over dry corn meal, butter and salt, blend well. Add eggs well beaten and remainder of milk. The batter must be very thin. Bake immediately in shallow, well buttered tins in a quick oven.

# CREAM CORN BREAD

| | |
|---|---|
| ¾ cup corn meal | 1 teaspoon salt |
| 1 cup white flour | 1 cup thick cream |
| 4 teaspoons baking powder | 2 eggs |
| 4 tablespoons sugar | 1 teaspoon butter or other fat |

PROCESS: Mix and sift the dry ingredients, add cream gradually stirring constantly, add melted shortening and eggs beaten until thick and lemon tinted. Pour mixture into a well greased, shallow pan and bake twenty-five minutes in a hot oven. If not brown on top, place some distance from the gas flame in the broiling oven until delicately browned. Care should be taken that cake does not burn during the browning process.

# CORN BREAD
## (New Orleans Recipe)

| | |
|---|---|
| 2 cups white corn meal | 2 tablespoons melted butter |
| ½ cup flour | 2 cups sour milk |
| ½ cup molasses or sugar | 1 teaspoon soda |
| 1 teaspoon salt | 2 eggs |

PROCESS: Sift together corn meal, flour and salt, add molasses and butter, and gradually sour milk while stirring constantly; add eggs beaten very light, then soda dissolved in two tablespoons hot water. Beat mixture thoroughly; bake slowly forty-five minutes in a well greased, shallow pan.

# SWEET CORN BREAD

| | |
|---|---|
| 1¾ cups flour | 1 teaspoon salt |
| ¾ cup corn meal | 2 eggs |
| ¼ cup melted butter | 1 cup milk |
| ½ cup sugar | 4 teaspoons baking powder |

PROCESS: Sift together flour, corn meal, salt and baking powder. Add sugar and melted butter; add milk gradually while stirring constantly. Beat the eggs until thick and lemon tinted; then fold carefully into first mixture. Turn into well buttered, shallow pan; bake twenty-five minutes in a hot oven. This mixture may be baked in hissing hot iron gem cups.

## OLD FASHION CORN BREAD
### (Southern Recipe)

| | |
|---|---|
| 1¾ cups corn meal (hand ground) | 2 tablespoons lard |
| 1 cup white flour | 1 egg |
| 1 teaspoon salt | 2 cups sour milk |
| 2 tablespoons sugar | 1 teaspoon soda |

PROCESS: Mix thoroughly corn meal, flour, salt and sugar. Rub in lard with tips of fingers. Add egg unbeaten and one and one-half cups sour milk; dissolve soda in remaining half cup of milk and stir mixture until ingredients are well blended; then beat (with the hand) six minutes. Turn into a well greased, shallow agate pan and bake thirty minutes in a fairly hot oven. Brown under the gas flame in broiling oven. This corn meal is coarse and should not be sifted. It is ground in a hand mill and contains all the good of the kernels.

# CRACKLING CORN BREAD

2 cups scalded milk  
1 cup corn meal  

2 teaspoons salt  
1 cup cracklings  

PROCESS: Pour scalded milk gradually over corn meal mixed with salt. stirring constantly; add cracklings and mix thoroughly. Turn into a well greased, shallow pan to the depth of one-half inch. Bake in a moderate oven until crisp and brown. Split and spread with butter. Serve hot. Cracklings are the residue from the trying out of lard. They are extensively used as food by the colored people of the South and by the Mexicans. Cracklings serve the purpose of shortening and as such have quite a food value. The prejudice against their use is chiefly because of their cheapness, as well as the erroneous idea that prevails among the people of the North especially, that "cracklings is refuse."

# KNOXVILLE CORN BREAD

1⅓ cups yellow corn meal  
⅓ cup flour  
1 cup rich sour milk  
¾ teaspoon soda (generous)  
1½ tablespoons butter  

½ teaspoon salt  
4 tablespoons sugar  
2 cups sweet milk  
2 eggs  

PROCESS: Sift together corn meal and flour. Add to sour milk soda, salt, sugar and eggs beaten until thick and lemon tinted and one cup of sweet milk. Add to corn meal slowly while stirring constantly. Melt butter in a No. 8 cast iron spider; turn in mixture, then slowly pour over remaining cup sweet milk. Bake in a hot oven thirty-five minutes. Reduce heat, if browning too fast. Cut like a pie and serve hot with butter and jam or maple syrup. This is a most delicious corn bread and is known in Knoxville as Mollie White's corn bread. Mollie White was a "famed" colored cook of that city.

**SKIMMED MILK AND BUTTER SUBSTITUTE MAY BE USED IN ALL RECIPES EXCEPT THOSE CALLING FOR CREAM.**

# SPIDER CORN CAKE

¾ cup corn meal  
¼ cup flour  
2 tablespoons sugar  
1 teaspoon salt  
1 teaspoon soda  

½ cup sweet milk  
1 egg well beaten  
½ cup sour milk  
2 tablespoons melted butter  
⅓ cup sweet milk  

PROCESS:  Sift together corn meal, flour, sugar, salt and soda.  Add half cup sweet milk and egg well beaten.  Add sour milk and butter.  Mix thoroughly and pour into well buttered hot spider.  Pour half cup sweet milk carefully over the top of corn cake.  Cook ten minutes on top of range and twenty minutes in the oven.

# ALABAMA PUMPKIN CORN BREAD

1½ cups corn meal  
½ cup graham flour  
1 teaspoon salt  
3 teaspoons baking powder  
½ cup soft brown sugar  

1 tablespoon hot water  
2 cups canned pumpkin  
¼ teaspoon soda  
1 egg  
1 cup milk  

PROCESS: Sift together corn meal, salt, baking powder; add graham flour unsifted.  Add sugar and hot water to pumpkin, sift in soda and add egg beaten until thick and lemon tinted.  Add pumpkin mixture to dry ingredients and beat until thoroughly blended, add milk and continue beating.  Turn into a buttered, shallow pan and bake thirty minutes in a hot oven.  This is an old southern recipe and when made by the "old colored mammy" who originated the bread she "cooked down" her own pumpkin and used white flour instead of graham flour.

## WHITE CORN MEAL BREAD

4 tablespoons butter  
⅛ cup sugar  
1½ cups milk  
1½ cups white corn meal  
1¼ cups flour  
4 teaspoons baking powder  
1 teaspoon salt  
Whites 3 eggs

PROCESS: Cream the butter, add the sugar gradually, sift the dry ingredients together twice and add to first mixture alternately with milk. Beat whites of eggs until stiff; cut and fold them into mixture. Bake in shallow, buttered pan twenty-five minutes.

## MOLASSES CORN BREAD

1 cup corn meal  
¾ cup flour  
1½ tablespoons baking powder  
1 teaspoon salt  
¼ cup molasses  
¾ cup skimmed milk  
1 egg  
2 tablespoons sausage or bacon fat

PROCESS: Sift together dry ingredients; add molasses and milk mixed together, stirring constantly. Beat egg until thick and lemon tinted add to first mixture. Add fat and beat two minutes. Bake in a well greased, shallow pan in a hot oven twenty-five minutes.

## THIN CORN BREAD

¾ cup yellow corn meal  
1¼ cups flour  
2 tablespoons sugar  
5 teaspoons baking powder  
¾ teaspoon salt  
1 cup thin cream  
1 egg well beaten  
2 tablespoons melted butter

PROCESS: Mix and sift the dry ingredients; add cream, beaten egg and butter, beat thoroughly; bake in a well greased, shallow pan, in a hot oven, twenty-five minutes; five minutes before removing from over brush over with milk to give it a richer color. Serve with baked or broiled fish.

**SKIMMED MILK AND BUTTER SUBSTITUTE MAY BE USED IN ALL RECIPES EXCEPT THOSE CALLING FOR CREAM.**

# EGGLESS CORN BREAD NO. 1

¾ cup corn meal  
¾ cup flour  
2 tablespoons sugar  
1½ tablespoons bacon or sausage fat  

¾ teaspoon salt  
¾ teaspoon soda  
1½ cups sour milk  

PROCESS: Sift together the first five ingredients; add sour milk slowly, stirring constantly until batter is smooth. Add bacon fat, beat one minute, then turn into a well greased, square, shallow pan eight inches square and bake in a hot oven twenty-five minutes. Brown over top by placing pan in broiling oven under gas flame. Broiler should be placed on bottom of oven.

# EGGLESS CORN BREAD NO. 2

1 cup corn meal  
⅜ cup flour  
2 tablespoons sugar  
2 tablespoons shortening  

1 teaspoon salt  
1 teaspoon soda  
1½ cups sour milk or butter-  
 milk  

PROCESS: Sift together the dry ingredients. Add milk gradually stirring constantly. Beat mixture one minute. Turn into a well greased, shallow pan and bake twenty-five minutes in a hot oven. If not brown on top place some distance from the gas flame in broiling oven for two minutes until evenly browned.

# SPONGE CORN CAKE NO. 1

½ cup corn meal  
1 cup flour  
½ teaspoon salt  
½ teaspoon soda  
5 tablespoons sugar  

2 egg yokes beaten very light  
1 tablespoon melted butter  
1 cup rich sour milk  
White 1 egg  

PROCESS: Sift the dry ingredients together, add butter, yolks well beaten and sour milk; lastly fold in the white of egg beaten until stiff. Bake in well greased, shallow pan in hot oven thirty minutes.

# SPONGE CAKE NO. 2

1 cup corn meal  
½ cup flour  
½ teaspoon salt  
½ teaspoon soda  
1 teaspoon cream tartar  

1 tablespoon melted butter  
4 tablespoons sugar  
2 egg yolks  
1 white of egg  
1¼ cups sweet milk  

PROCESS: Sift the dry ingredients together, add butter, egg yolks well beaten, and milk; mix well and lastly cut and fold in the white of egg beaten until stiff. Bake in well greased, brick-shaped bread pan, thirty minutes.

# OLD VIRGINIA BATTER BREAD

2 cups corn meal  
4 cups scalded milk  
1 teaspoon salt  

½ cup sugar  
3 eggs  

PROCESS: Stir corn meal into scalded milk and cook to a mush, add salt and sugar, cool; add yolks of eggs beaten very light; then cut and fold in whites beaten until stiff, melt two tablespoons butter or lard in baking pan, turn in mixture and bake forty-five minutes in a bread oven (360 to 400 degrees F.).

SKIMMED MILK AND BUTTER SUBSTITUTE MAY BE USED IN ALL RECIPES EXCEPT THOSE CALLING FOR CREAM.

# CORN PONE

To two cups corn meal (water milled) add one and one-half teaspoons salt and one tablespoon bacon fat or melted lard and sufficient scalded milk or equal parts of milk and boiling water to make a mixture that can be molded with the hands into oblong cakes six inches long, three inches wide and one inch thick in center; the pones should taper at the ends and a trifle thinner.  Before molding, the mixture (when cool enough) should be thoroughly blended with the hand; then shaped, placed on a hot, well greased tin baking sheet, brushed over with melted fat or milk and baked twenty-five minutes in a hot oven.  When done, split each pone, spread with butter and lay a thin slice of broiled bacon between; fold again and serve immediately.

## MAMMY'S PUMPKIN PONE

2 cups corn meal  
2 cups cooked and strained or  
  canned pumpkin  

1 teaspoon salt  
⅛ cup sugar  
2 tablespoons sausage fat

PROCESS:  Mix ingredients in the order given. Beat vigorously until thoroughly blended, then slightly butter the hands and mold the mixture into pones almost an inch thick in the middle.  Place on a well greased baking sheet and bake thirty minutes in a hot oven. Split, butter them, and serve at once.

# KENTUCKY SPOON CORN BREAD

1 cup corn meal  
2 cups cold cooked rice  
1 tablespoon butter  
1 ½ cups milk  

1 teaspoon salt  
2 eggs well beaten  
1 teaspoon baking powder  

PROCESS: Wet corn meal with boiling water and stir until the consistency of mush, add rice, butter and salt; let stand over night or several hours during the day. Then add eggs and milk; sift baking powder into mixture. Beat well and pour into a well buttered, shallow pudding dish; bake thirty-five minutes in a moderate oven. Dot over with small bits of butter when almost done. Serve with a spoon from dish in which it was baked.

# RICE AND CORN MEAL SPOON BREAD

½ cup rice  
2 ½ cups boiling water  
½ teaspoon salt  
3 tablespoons butter or butterine  

3 eggs  
¾ cup skimmed milk  
1 ¼ cups white corn meal  
3 teaspoons baking powder  
Cheese sauce  

PROCESS: Blanch rice; add to boiling water; add salt and cook five minutes, stirring constantly. Then cook in double boiler until rice is tender. Remove from range, add butter, eggs beaten until thick and lemon tinted; add milk gradually with corn meal sifted with baking powder. Beat mixture thoroughly and turn into a well greased baking dish and bake in a moderate oven forty-five minutes. Serve from the baking dish with a spoon. Cheese sauce may be served with this bread and will supply the needs of a Meatless Day for dinner.

**SKIMMED MILK AND BUTTER SUBSTITUTE MAY BE USED IN ALL RECIPES EXCEPT THOSE CALLING FOR CREAM.**

# VIRGINIA SPOON CORN BREAD

| | |
|---|---|
| ½ cup granulated cooked hominy | 3 eggs |
| 1 teaspoon salt | 1 ½ cups milk |
| 2 tablespoons lard | 2 cups corn meal |
| 2 tablespoons butter | 2 teaspoons baking powder |

PROCESS: Add shortening and salt to hot hominy, add corn meal sifted with baking powder, alternately with milk, mix well. Beat eggs until thick and lemon tinted; add to first mixture and beat vigorously. Pour into a well buttered pudding dish, bake in hot oven forty-five minutes. Serve in baking dish with spoon.

# CUSTARD CORN CAKE

| | |
|---|---|
| ½ cup corn meal | 2 tablespoons sugar |
| ½ cup bread flour | 1 cup sour or buttermilk |
| ½ teaspoon salt | 2 eggs |
| ½ teaspoon soda | 2 tablespoons melted lard or |
| ½ cup sweet milk | butter |

PROCESS: Sift together corn meal, flour, salt, soda and sugar. Add sour milk, gradually stirring constantly; add eggs beaten until thick and lemon tinted, continue beating until thoroughly blended. Put melted shortening into a warm earthen baking dish (one quart capacity). Beat batter one minute and turn into dish, pouring the sweet milk over top. Bake twenty-five minutes in a hot oven. Cut as a pie and serve at once from the dish in which it was baked.

# APPLE JOHNNY CAKE

2 cups white or yellow corn meal
2 tablespoons sugar
½ teaspoon salt
1 teaspoon soda
1 teaspoon cream of tartar or

4 teaspoons baking powder
1¾ cups milk
3 sour apples
½ cup milk (extra)
Cinnamon and sugar

PROCESS: Sift together the first five ingredients in the order given; add milk gradually and beat until batter is smooth. Pare, core and thinly slice apples; stir them into first mixture. Turn into a well buttered, shallow pan; spread evenly and pour over the extra half cup of cold milk. Sprinkle top with cinnamon and sugar. Bake thirty-five minutes in a hot oven. This cake is delicious if made with "water-milled" corn meal. Serve hot as a dessert with sweetened cream or with butter as corn bread.

# LUNCHEON JOHNNY CAKE

Yolks 4 eggs
2 tablespoons butter
2 cups milk (not skimmed)
2 cups corn meal

1 cup flour
1 teaspoon salt
2 tablespoons sugar
4 teaspoons baking powder
Whites 4 eggs

PROCESS: Beat yolks until thick and light; add milk gradually; stir into meal and flour sifted with salt, sugar and baking powder, beat thoroughly. Add butter and carefully fold in the whites of eggs beaten until stiff. Turn into a well greased, shallow pan and bake forty minutes in a moderate oven. Serve hot with maple syrup or orange marmalade for luncheon. With a glass of milk or a cup of cocoa the luncheon is complete.

**SKIMMED MILK AND BUTTER SUBSTITUTE MAY BE USED IN ALL RECIPES EXCEPT THOSE CALLING FOR CREAM.**

# BLUEBERRY CORN BREAD

1 cup corn meal — ½ teaspoon salt
1 cup pastry flour — 1 egg well beaten
4 teaspoons baking powder — ¾ cup milk
1 cup sugar — ¼ cup melted butter
½ cup blueberries dredged with a little of the flour

PROCESS: Sift together the dry ingredients; add milk gradually and beaten egg. Add butter and berries. Bake in a well buttered, shallow pan or in well greased, hot iron muffin cups, twenty-five minutes in a hot oven. Serve hot as it is then at its best.

# CORN BREAD WITH CREAMED CLAMS

1 quart fresh clams — White corn bread
2 cups white sauce — *(Recipe on Page 58)*
¼ pound fat salt pork — Butter

PROCESS: Remove the tough portion from the clams and finely chop. Cut salt pork in one-fourth-inch dice; try out in a hot frying pan. Drain off some of the fat, leaving enough to prevent clams from sticking to bottom of pan; add soft and chopped hard part of clams, stir until heated through; add white sauce and heat to boiling point. Remove at once from fire. Have ready a hot white corn bread made from recipe on Page 58. Cut corn bread in squares, split each square and spread half the squares with butter, cover with part of the clam mixture, set the other halves above and pour around or over remaining clam mixture. Serve very hot.

# CHAPTER IV.

### BOILED GREEN CORN

Remove the outer husks; strip back the inner ones. Pick out all the silky threads, fold back the husks and cook corn in boiling, salted water from ten to twenty minutes, according to age of corn. Add salt last ten minutes of cooking. Drain well and serve on platter in napkin, folding the corners over the corn.

### GREEN CORN COOKED IN MILK

Follow recipe for Boiled Green Corn, using equal parts of skimmed milk and water. Salt the milk and water five minutes before removing corn. Drain; serve in folded napkin.

### ROASTED GREEN CORN

Remove the husks and all the silk from freshly gathered sweet corn, preferably Golden Bantam. Brush over lightly with melted butter or bacon fat. Arrange side by side on the broiler and place some distance from the flame in the broiling oven of the gas range. As the kernels brown, turn the ears until evenly browned all over. Brush again with butter, dredge lightly with salt and pepper and serve on a hot platter in the folds of a large napkin.

SKIMMED MILK AND BUTTER SUBSTITUTE MAY BE USED IN ALL
RECIPES EXCEPT THOSE CALLING FOR CREAM.

## TO SWEETEN GREEN CORN WHEN BOILING

When boiling green corn on the cobs; to supply the natural sweetness lost by evaporation after being pulled from the stalk, add two tablespoons of sugar to the water in which the corn is cooked and a luscious flavor will be developed. Salt should never be added to the water in which corn is boiled as the salt has a tendency to darken and harden the kernels.

## STEAMED GREEN CORN ON THE COBS

For steaming green corn on the cobs; if possible have the corn freshly gathered. Remove the outer husks, turn back the inner husks and pick off every thread of silk. Turn back the husks in their original place and arrange ears in a steamer. Place over a kettle of boiling water and steam fifteen minutes (twenty minutes if ears are large). Remove from steamer and quickly pull off the husks and arrange ears in a folded napkin on a warm serving platter. Serve at once. This is an ideal way of cooking green corn as nothing is lost in the cooking process.

## CORN WITH CREAM

Cut corn from cob while hot. There should be two cups. Turn into saucepan and season with salt, pepper and one teaspoon sugar; add one and one-half tablespoons butter or strained bacon fat and three tablespoons cream; reheat and serve. When cutting corn from cob do not cut so deep that portions of cob are cut off with corn. The better way is to score the kernels lengthwise of the cob, then press out pulp with the back of a silver knife, leaving the hulls on the cob.

**SKIMMED MILK AND BUTTER SUBSTITUTE MAY BE USED IN ALL RECIPES EXCEPT THOSE CALLING FOR CREAM.**

# FRIED GREEN CORN

Cut the corn from cob, using care that none of the cob is cut with it. Melt butter in a spider, add corn, separate the kernels and stir until corn is delicately browned; use as little butter as possible; strained bacon fat may be used instead of butter; season with salt pepper and a little rich cream. Do not allow mixture to boil after cream is added. Serve with chicken croquettes.

# STEWED GREEN CORN

Cut the corn from one dozen ears of tender, green corn. Put the corn in a saucepan, add sufficient water to cover; bring to boiling point and cook twenty minutes. There should be very little moisture left. Add one-half cup cream or top milk, one teaspoon sugar, one tablespoon butter and season with pepper and salt. For a change use equal parts of corn and tomatoes; season the same. Tomatoes should be peeled, cut in quarters and seeds scraped out. Cook until tender with the corn.

# GREEN CORN CREOLE

6 ears tender sweet green corn  
1 tablespoon olive oil or melted butter  
1 medium sized green pepper finely chopped  
1 medium sized onion finely chopped  
2 tomatoes peeled and finely chopped  
½ teaspoon salt  
1 teaspoon sugar  
¼ teaspoon paprika  
1 small clove garlic

PROCESS: Score each row of kernels lengthwise of the cobs. With the back of the knife press out pulp, leaving hulls on the cobs. Heat oil or butter in a saucepan, add pepper and onion; cook until delicately browned, stirring constantly. Add corn pulp, mix thoroughly and cook eight minutes, stirring lightly meanwhile; add tomatoes and seasoning and continue cooking ten minutes. Thrust a small wooden skewer (tooth-pick) through a small clove of garlic, drop it into mixture and stir lightly until a delicate flavor is imparted to mixture. Remove garlic (the skewer will help to locate garlic). Turn into a hot serving dish and serve with roast veal, beef, pork or fried chicken.

## SUCCOTASH

Cut hot, boiled corn from the cob; there should be one cup; add equal quantity of hot, boiled lima beans, the latter cooked in boiling, salted water or white stock. Dot over with one or two tablespoons butter, season with salt and pepper. A tablespoon of top milk may be added to supply moisture.

# SOUTHERN SUCCOTASH

6 ears green corn
2 cups green lima beans

¼ pound salt pork
1 tablespoon sugar
Salt and pepper

PROCESS: Cut the corn carefully from the cob. Put the cobs into water to cover; let them boil twenty minutes. Remove the cobs and strain the liquor over the cut corn; add the beans and salt pork cut in half-inch cubes; add sugar and season with salt and pepper. Let simmer slowly one hour until the moisture is evaporated to the desired consistency. In the south this dish resembles soup somewhat. It is more generally liked, however, served as a vegetable about the consistency of stewed corn; two or three tablespoons of hot cream added just before serving is an addition to this dish.

# SUCCOTASH WITH TOMATOES

1 cup cooked corn
1 cup cooked shelled beans
4 tomatoes sliced
½ green pepper finely chopped

1 small onion finely chopped
2 tablespoons butter
½ tablespoon sugar
1 teaspoon salt
Few grains cayenne

PROCESS: Melt butter in a saucepan, add chopped onion and pepper; cook without browning until soft, stirring constantly. Score the kernels lengthwise of the cobs of left-over corn, then measure. Shell and cook the beans that have become ripe in boiling, salted water; drain; combine with corn; add sliced tomatoes, cooked onion and pepper. Add seasoning and sugar. Cook until tomato is soft and the mixture is slightly thickened. Serve hot with roast veal, beef or pork.

# CORN A LA MEXICAN

| | |
|---|---|
| 6 tomatoes | ¾ teaspoon salt |
| 2 tablespoons butter | 2 cups hot green corn |
| 1 green pepper finely chopped | 1 tablespoon butter or cream |
| 1 small clove garlic or 1 teaspoon finely chopped onion | |

PROCESS: Cut tomatoes in quarters, scrape out all the seeds. Melt butter in saucepan, add pepper and garlic; cook without browning, three minutes; add tomatoes and salt; cook five minutes; add corn freshly boiled and cut from the cob; add a tablespoon of butter or cream and serve. Before chopping pepper, cover with boiling water, let stand one minute, then peel off the tissue-like skin covering it. Pimentos may be used when green peppers are not available.

# CORN SOUTHERN STYLE

| | |
|---|---|
| 2 cups cooked corn or 1 can of corn | ⅛ teaspoon pepper |
| | 1 teaspoon sugar |
| 2 eggs slightly beaten | 1 ½ tablespoons melted butter |
| 1 teaspoon salt | 2 cups scalded milk |

PROCESS: Mix the ingredients in the order given, turn mixture into a buttered pudding dish and bake until mixture is firm. Serve with fried chicken, roast veal, pork or beef.

# SWEET CORN—NEW ENGLAND STYLE

Finely chop one can of corn or two cups of green corn. Add three eggs slightly beaten, one-half tablespoon sugar, one teaspoon salt, one-eighth teaspoon pepper, one tablespoon melted butter and two cups scalded milk. Turn into a buttered baking dish or into individual ramekins and bake in a slow oven until solid or like custard. Serve in baking dish.

## SCALLOPED CORN

1 small mild green pepper  
1 small onion finely chopped  
2 tablespoons butter or butter substitute  
2 tablespoons flour  
1 teaspoon salt  
¼ teaspoon paprika  

Few grains cayenne  
½ cup milk  
1½ cups canned corn  
Yolk 1 egg  
1½ tablespoons butter or bacon fat  
½ cup tiny stale bread cubes  
¾ cup cracker crumbs  

PROCESS: Cut pepper in halves; remove seeds and veins; cut in narrow strips and strips in halves crosswise. Mix with onion and cook both with butter five minutes, stirring constantly. Sift together flour and seasonings; add to first mixture and stir until well blended; then add milk gradually, continue stirring. Bring to boiling point, add corn, yolk of egg slightly beaten. Brown bread cubes in remaining butter and add to mixture. Turn into a buttered baking dish, cover with buttered cracker crumbs and bake in a hot oven until heated through and crumbs are browned.

# STEWED CORN AND TOMATOES

Cut the corn from the cobs of six ears of tender, sweet green corn; scrape the cobs with back of knife. Cook until tender in as little water as possible, then add an equal quantity of stewed tomatoes. Add one-third cup butter and one tablespoon sugar. Season with salt and pepper, heat to boiling point and turn into hot serving dish. This mixture may be turned into a buttered baking dish, the top covered with buttered and seasoned crumbs, then placed in the oven until crumbs are browned.

## CORN FRITTERS NO. 1

1 cup canned corn  
1 well beaten egg  

¼ cup flour  
1 teaspoon sugar  
Salt and pepper

PROCESS: Mix corn, flour and sugar together, add well beaten egg, season highly with salt and pepper and drop on well buttered hot griddle about the size of N. Y. Counts. Brown on one side and then turn and brown the other. Serve with fried chicken or chicken croquettes.

## CORN FRITTERS NO. 2

1 cup corn cut from cob  
1 cup flour  
1 teaspoon salt  
Few grains cayenne  

1 teaspoon sugar  
½ cup milk  
1 tablespoon olive oil  
1 egg lightly beaten

PROCESS: Beat egg thoroughly; add remaining ingredients in order given. Drop by tablespoonfuls into deep, hot fat. Cook six to eight minutes, turning often. Drain on brown paper and serve surrounding broiled chicken. These fritters may be cooked on a well greased, hissing hot griddle as Corn Fritters No. 1.

# SWEET CORN FRITTERS NO. 3

1 cup sweet green corn pulp  
2 eggs  
½ teaspoon salt  
⅛ teaspoon pepper  
1 teaspoon sugar  
1 cup pastry flour  
1½ teaspoons baking powder  
Whites 2 eggs

PROCESS: With a sharp knife score the kernels of Golden Bantam corn lengthwise of the cob; with the back of knife press out the pulp; then measure. To pulp add the yolks of eggs beaten until thick and light, then the seasonings. Add flour sifted with baking powder. Then fold in the whites of eggs beaten until stiff. Drop by rounded tablespoons into hot fat, fry until evenly browned, turning often while frying. Drain on brown paper and serve at once.

# CORN AND CELERY FRITTERS

½ cup finely chopped canned corn  
½ cup finely chopped celery  
1 egg well beaten  
¼ cup flour  
1 teaspoon sugar  
Salt and pepper

PROCESS: Mix ingredients in the order given. Mix thoroughly. Drop by small spoonfuls on a hissing hot, well greased griddle. Brown on one side, turn and brown the other. These fritters should be about the size of individual butter plates.

# CORN AND OYSTER FRITTERS

| | |
|---|---|
| 1 cup canned corn | ⅓ cup cream or rich milk |
| 1 egg well beaten | ½ cup pastry flour |
| ½ teaspoon salt | ½ teaspoon baking powder |
| ½ teaspoon white pepper | 1 cup oysters |

PROCESS:  Chop corn very fine, add ingredients in the order given (except oysters).  Mix thoroughly. Bring oysters to the boiling point in their own liquor; let cook one minute, drain and dry them between towels. Take up a tablespoonful of the batter, make a depression in center, lay an oyster in it, sprinkle with salt and pepper; cover with more batter.  With a small spatula or teaspoon scrape the fritter into a well greased, hissing hot frying pan; repeat until there are as many fritters in pan as can be conveniently turned.  Let fritters cook until browned on one side, then turn and brown the other side.  There should be plenty of fat in pan.  Tried-out fat, salt pork fat is best for this purpose.

# CORN OYSTERS

| | |
|---|---|
| 2 cups green corn pulp | ½ teaspoon sugar |
| 1 tablespoon melted butter | 2 eggs well beaten |
| ¼ teaspoon salt | Pepper and flour |

PROCESS:  With a sharp knife cut through the kernels lengthwise of the cob; scrape out the pulp with the back of a silver knife; add butter, seasoning, eggs, and lastly sufficient flour to shape in small cakes the size of N. Y. Counts.  Saute in tried-out salt pork fat or butter.  Brown on one side, then turn and brown the other side.

# VIRGINIA CORN CAKES

¾ cup grated green or canned
  corn
½ cup milk
1 ½ teaspoon sugar

2 eggs
⅞ cup flour
3 teaspoons baking powder
½ teaspoon salt

PROCESS:  If canned corn is used it should be finely chopped.  To corn pulp add milk, sugar and eggs, beaten until thick and lemon tinted.  Sift together flour, baking powder and salt.  Combine mixtures.  Put a tablespoon of mixture into buttered muffin rings arranged in a buttered dripping pan.  Bake in a moderate oven, fifteen minutes.  Serve with roast veal, beef or pork.

## GREEN PEPPERS STUFFED WITH GREEN CORN

Cut a slice from the stem ends of the required number of firm, green peppers of uniform size; remove veins and seeds.   Score the kernels of tender, sweet corn lengthwise of the cob and press out pulp with the back of knife.  Season corn pulp with salt, paprika, a little cream, melted butter and chopped chives.  Fill peppers with mixture; cover tops with buttered crumbs.  Arrange peppers in a buttered baking dish and bake in a moderate oven until peppers are soft. Two tablespoons of the slices of green pepper finely chopped and sauted in one tablespoon of bacon fat or butter five minutes may be added to corn mixture if desired.

# TOMATOES STUFFED WITH SUCCOTASH

Wash, wipe and remove a thin slice from the stem end of six uniform-sized tomatoes, scoop out the inside, sprinkle with salt, invert, let stand one-half hour. Mix the pulp with one cup of succotash, stuff tomatoes and arrange them in a granite dripping pan well greased; sprinkle the top of each with buttered cracker crumbs. Bake in hot oven twenty minutes or until tender. Baste once with melted bacon fat or butter substitute. Serve with roast loin of veal.

# TOMATOES STUFFED WITH GREEN CORN

Cut a slice from the stem ends of the required number of firm tomatoes of uniform size; reserve slices. Scoop out pulp and seeds; score the kernels of tender sweet corn lengthwise of cob and press out pulp with back of knife. Sprinkle the inside of tomatoes with a little salt. Season corn pulp with salt, paprika, melted butter, cream and chopped chives or onion juice. Fill tomatoes with mixture, set the slices cut from stem ends in place. Arrange tomatoes in a buttered baking dish and bake in a moderate oven until tomatoes are soft. A green pepper finely chopped and sauted in butter five minutes may be added to the corn if desired.

# GREEN CORN AU GRATIN

1 tablespoon finely chopped onion  
1 tablespoon finely chopped green pepper  
1 tablespoon butter  
2 tablespoons flour  
½ teaspoon salt  
2 cups rich milk or thin cream  
Green corn cut from cob  
2 eggs  
Buttered cracker crumbs

PROCESS: Cook onion and pepper in butter until soft but browned; add flour mixed with salt and stir until smooth; add milk or cream gradually, stirring constantly until boiling point is reached. Add enough sweet green corn to make a consistent mixture; add eggs lightly beaten. Turn mixture into a well greased, individual ramekins; cover with buttered cracker crumbs and bake in the oven until heated through and crumbs are browned. Serve as an entree or as the main dish at luncheon or supper.

# CREAMED CORN AU GRATIN

4 tablespoons butter or butter substitute  
4 tablespoons flour  
1 teaspoon salt  
⅛ teaspoons white pepper  
Few grains cayenne  
1 teaspoon sugar  
1½ cups rich milk  
2 cups green corn cut from cob  
¾ cup cracker crumbs  
¼ cup melted butter or butter substitute

PROCESS: Melt fat in a saucepan; add flour, salt, pepper, sugar and gradually milk, stirring constantly. Cook one minute; then stir in corn; bring to boiling point; then turn into a buttered baking dish; cover top with cracker crumbs mixed with melted fat and bake twenty minutes ·in a moderate oven.

SKIMMED MILK AND BUTTER SUBSTITUTE MAY BE USED IN ALL
RECIPES EXCEPT THOSE CALLING FOR CREAM.

# CORN CROQUETTES

1 quart grated green corn  
2 cups milk  
2 tablespoons butter  
2 tablespoons cheese  
1 teaspoon salt  
¼ teaspoon pepper  
1 teaspoon sugar  
2 well beaten eggs  
3 tablespoons flour

PROCESS:  Cook corn and flour in milk in double boiler twenty minutes; add butter, cheese, salt, pepper, sugar and well beaten eggs; spread in granite dripping pan to the depth of one inch.  When cold cut in two-inch squares, dip in flour, egg and cracker crumbs;  fry in deep fat.  Drain on brown paper and serve with fried chicken.

# CORN TIMBALES

2 tablespoons butter or butter substitute  
2 tablespoons chopped onion  
2 tablespoons chopped green pepper  
2 cups hot green corn or 1 can corn  
½ cup soft bread crumbs  
1 teaspoon sugar  
1 teaspoon salt  
⅛ teaspoon pepper  
3 eggs

PROCESS:  Melt fat in a saucepan, add onion and pepper, cook five minutes without browning, stir constantly, add corn finely chopped, bread crumbs, sugar, salt and pepper; beat the egg yolks thick and light; add to first mixture; cut and fold in the whites beaten until stiff.  Fill well buttered timbale molds two-thirds full; set molds in pan of hot water and bake until mixture is firm.  Serve with tomato sauce.

# CORN CUSTARD

1 cup cooked green corn or canned corn finely chopped  
4 eggs slightly beaten  
½ teaspoon salt  
1 teaspoon sugar  
⅛ teaspoon pepper  
Few drops onion juice  
1¼ cups scalded milk  

PROCESS: Beat eggs slightly, add seasoning and pour on slowly scalded milk; continue beating; add corn, mix well; turn into a buttered baking dish set in a pan of hot water; bake in moderate oven twenty to twenty-five minutes. Stir mixture once while cooking to prevent corn from settling to the bottom of dish. Turn on serving platter and surround with broiled tomatoes.

# KORNLET CUSTARD

3 eggs slightly beaten  
1 teaspoon sugar  
½ teaspoon salt  
⅛ teaspoon white pepper  
½ can kornlet  
2 cups milk  
Onion juice  

PROCESS: To the slightly beaten eggs add sugar, salt, pepper, kornlet and gradually the milk and flavor with onion juice. Stir until well mixed. Turn into a buttered baking dish, set dish in a pan of boiling water and bake in a moderate oven until firm. Serve from baking dish at luncheon or supper.

# CORN OMELET

4 eggs beaten separately  
4 tablespoons hot water  
1 teaspoon salt  
⅛ teaspoon pepper  

1 teaspoon sugar  
1½ tablespoons butter  
½ cup corn cut from the cob  
   or canned corn  

PROCESS: Beat the yolks of eggs until thick and light; add salt, pepper, sugar, corn and hot water; mix well. Beat whites of eggs until stiff and cut and fold them into first mixture; blend thoroughly. Melt butter in iron spider; tip it so the sides are well buttered; turn in the mixture, spread evenly; cook ten minutes on top of range; then finish cooking in the oven. Fold as puffy omelet on a hot platter. Serve with thin white cheese or tomato sauce.

# GREEN CORN PUDDING

2 cups grated cooked green corn  
2 eggs slightly beaten  
¼ cup melted butter  

¼ cup milk  
1 teaspoon sugar  
Salt, pepper  

PROCESS: Grate the corn from the cobs or score each row of kernels lengthwise of cob and press out pulp with the back of knife. There should be two cups. To corn pulp add eggs slightly beaten, melted butter, milk and seasonings. Turn into a buttered baking dish and bake until firm. Test by thrusting silver knife into pudding; if knife comes out clean, pudding is done. Serve as a vegetable.

# CORN PUDDING

Yolks 3 eggs  
2 cups green corn  
2 cups milk  
⅛ cup butter  
Whites 3 eggs  
Salt and pepper

PROCESS: Beat yolks of eggs until thick and light; add corn, milk, butter, salt and pepper to taste. Fold in whites of eggs beaten until stiff; turn into a buttered pudding dish and bake in a moderate oven one hour.

# GREEN CORN SCRAMBLED WITH EGGS

3 small ears of cooked corn or  
⅛ can of corn  
1 teaspoon salt  
1½ tablespoons bacon fat or butter  
⅛ teaspoon white pepper  
1 tablespoon finely chopped green pepper  
4 eggs sl'ghtly beaten

PROCESS: Use Golden Bantam corn if possible. Cut corn from cob and mix with salt, pepper and green pepper. Melt fat in an omelet pan; add corn mixture and cook three minutes; add eggs. Stir and scrape carefully from the bottom of pan and cook until eggs are set. Roll on to a hot serving platter, sprinkle with paprika and garnish with crisp bacon and sprigs of parsley.

# GREEN CORN WAFFLES

1¼ cups flour  
1½ tablespoons baking powder  
½ teaspoon salt  
Yolks 3 eggs  
⅔ cup green corn pulp  
½ cup cream  
¼ cup butter  
Whites 3 eggs

PROCESS: Sift together the dry ingredients. Beat yolk of eggs until thick and lemon tinted; add to cream and gradually stir into dry ingredients. Add corn pulp and melted butter. Beat thoroughly; then fold in the whites of eggs beaten until stiff. Cook at once in a hot, well greased waffle iron.

**SKIMMED MILK AND BUTTER SUBSTITUTE MAY BE USED IN ALL RECIPES EXCEPT THOSE CALLING FOR CREAM.**

# GREEN CORN GRIDDLE CAKES NO. 1

1 cup grated cold cooked green corn
2 tablespoons melted butter or
   bacon fat
1 tablespoon sugar

2½ cups flour
2 teaspoons baking powder
1 egg lightly beaten
2 cups sweet milk

PROCESS: Add butter, salt and sugar to grated corn; sift flour and baking powder together; add to first mixture alternately with the milk; add lightly beaten egg and cook as griddle cakes on a hot, well greased griddle.

# GREEN CORN GRIDDLE CAKES NO. 2

2 cups cold cooked grated corn
1 cup flour
1 teaspoon salt

1 teaspoon baking powder
2 teaspoons sugar
½ cup top milk
2 eggs

PROCESS: Grate the corn from the cobs or cut from cobs and finely chop. Sift together flour, salt, baking powder and sugar; add to corn pulp, mix thoroughly. Add milk and yolks of eggs well beaten. Beat whites of eggs until stiff; fold them into mixture; beat batter one minute. Cook as griddle cakes. If skimmed milk is used, add one tablespoon of melted butter.

# CORN AND BACON

12 thin slices bacon
2 cups canned corn or
  1 ½ cups dried corn
Salt, pepper and paprika

2 eggs
½ green pepper finely chopped
1 medium sized onion finely
  chopped

PROCESS:  Arrange slices of bacon in a cold iron skillet, heat slowly until most of the fat is tried out; drain off fat occasionally.  Increase meat and crisp bacon quickly without burning. Remove to warming oven. Cook pepper and onion in three tablespoons of the fat until soft without browning.  Add corn, stir until well mixed; add eggs lightly beaten, salt, pepper and paprika.  Scramble as scrambled eggs.  Heap in a mound on a hot platter and garnish with bacon.  If dried corn is used follow recipe for Cooking Dried Corn, and finish as directed in above recipe.

# CORN TOAST

½ tablespoon onion finely chopped
1 ½ tablespoons butter or butter
  substitute
1 cup canned corn

2 cups rich cream
½ teaspoon salt
¼ teaspoon paprika
6 rounds toasted bread

PROCESS:  Melt butter in a saucepan; add onion and cook three minutes without browning, stirring constantly.  Add corn, cream and seasonings, bring to boiling point and cook very slowly five minutes.  Arrange hot buttered toast on a hot platter.  Pour over mixture, sprinkle with paprika and grated cheese and serve immediately.

# CREAM OF CORN SOUP

| | |
|---|---|
| 1 can corn | 1 teaspoon sugar |
| 2 cups boiling water | 2 tablespoons butter |
| 2 cups scalded milk | 2 tablespoons flour |
| 1 slice onion | 1 teaspoon salt |
| | ⅛ teaspoon white pepper |

PROCESS: Finely chop the corn from one can; add boiling water, cook slowly twenty minutes. Scald milk with onions, remove onion and add milk to corn. Add sugar and bind with butter or butter substitute and flour cooked together. Add salt and pepper. Serve with freshly popped corn slightly salted.

# CORN SOUP WITH WHIPPED CREAM

| | |
|---|---|
| 6 ears or 1 can of corn | 1 teaspoon sugar |
| 2 cups cold water | 1½ teaspoons salt |
| 2 tablespoons finely chopped onion | 3 tablespoons butter or butter substitute |
| 2 cups scalded milk | 3 tablespoons flour |
| | 1 cup condensed cream, whipped |

PROCESS: Cut corn from cob, chop fine, add water and cook twenty minutes. Rub through a puree strainer; add scalded milk. Cook onion in·butter five minutes without browning; remove onion, add flour and cook one minute; add seasoning and corn mixture. Mix well, bring to boiling point, cook five minutes; then pour over whipped cream placed in bottom of hot soup tureen. Serve with crisp crackers.

# GREEN CORN SOUP

6 ears sweet green corn  
2 cups milk scalded with  
1 slice onion  
1 teaspoon sugar  

1 teaspoon salt  
⅛ teaspoon white pepper  
2 tablespoons flour  
2 tablespoons butter  
Paprika  

PROCESS: Grate the corn; there should be two cups pulp. Cover cobs with cold water and bring to boiling point and simmer thirty minutes. Strain the liquor; there should be two cups. To this liquor add the corn pulp and cook fifteen minutes, counting from time boiling point is reached. Add seasonings, remove onion from scalded milk or cream and add to corn mixture. Melt butter in a saucepan, add flour, stir to a smooth paste; add gradually some of the hot mixture until of the consistency to pour. Combine mixtures and cook five minutes. Sprinkle each portion with paprika and pass daintily browned cheese crackers.

# CORN SOUP WITH TOMATOES

2 cups grated cooked green corn  
  or 1 can corn  
1½ cups tomatoes  
½ green or red pepper  
1 tablespoon onion finely chopped  

1 small clove garlic finely  
  chopped  
6 cups well seasoned chicken  
  or veal stock  
Salt and pepper  

PROCESS: Peel and quarter tomatoes, scrape out all the seeds, add tomatoes, corn, pepper, onion and garlic to stock; place kettle on range, bring to boiling point, cook rapidly five minutes, reduce heat and simmer until vegetables are tender (about thirty minutes). Season with salt and pepper. Serve with croutons.

# CORN CHOWDER

2 cups cooked green corn or
  1 can corn
1 cup salt pork cut in half cubes
4 cups potatoes cut in ¼-inch
  cubes
½ onion sliced

2 cups boiling water
3 cups milk
3 tablespoons butter or
  butter substitute
4 Boston crackers
Salt, pepper and few grains
  cayenne

PROCESS: Try out the cubes of pork in saucepan; add onion and cook five minutes without browning; strain fat into stewpan. Parboil potato cubes five minutes; drain; add potatoes to fat; add two cups boiling water; continue cooking until potatoes are tender. Add corn and milk scalded, bring to boiling point. Season with salt, pepper and cayenne; add butter and crackers, the latter split and soaked in cold skimmed milk enough to cover. Remove crackers with skimmer, turn chowder into hot tureen, place crackers on top and serve immediately. A delicious chowder may be made by substituting the same quantity of succotash for the corn.

# CORN AND TOMATO SALAD

1 cup tomato pulp  
1 slice onion  
2 slices carrot  
1 blade celery broken in pieces  
1 sprig parsley  
Bit of bay leaf  
4 cloves  
¼ teaspoon pepper corns  

1 teaspoon salt  
1 teaspoon Worcestershire  
  sauce  
⅛ teaspoon soda  
1 cup freshly cooked or  
  canned corn (latter drained)  
1 tablespoon granulated  
  gelatine  
2 tablespoons cold water  

PROCESS:  Cook the first eight ingredients in a saucepan twenty minutes; then rub through a strainer; add soda, salt, Worcestershire and hot corn. Soak gelatine in cold water and dissolve over hot water. Remove first mixture from range; add gelatine, mix well and pour into individual molds previously wet in cold water. Chill thoroughly, unmold and serve in nests of lettuce leaves; garnish with Mayonnaise dressing.

# CORN SALAD

2 cups freshly boiled green corn  
½ green or red pepper  

4 young onions or 2 table-  
  spoons finely chopped chives  

PROCESS:  Cut tender, freshly cooked corn from the cob; add pepper and onion finely chopped; toss lightly and marinate with French dressing; let stand to ripen one hour; then serve in nests of endive with or without Mayonnaise dressing.

# CORN HASH
## (Relish to Serve with Meats, etc.)

½ small head cabbage  
2 green peppers  
1 cup sugar  
2 tablespoons whole mustard  
  seeds  
1 red pepper  

2 medium sized onions  
3 cups freshly cooked corn  
1 tablespoon whole black  
  pepper  
1 tablespoon celery seed  
Vinegar to cover  
Salt to taste  

PROCESS: Chop cabbage, peppers and onion very fine; add corn freshly boiled and cut from cob. Add sugar, mustard, celery seed and pepper. Mix well, season to taste with salt; add vinegar and simmer twenty minutes. Store in half-pint glass jars in a cool place.

## CORN RELISH

14 ears sweet green corn  
½ medium sized head white  
  cabbage  
3 green peppers  
2 mild red peppers  
3 large onions  
½ teaspoon celery seed  

¼ cup salt  
1½ cups granulated sugar  
6 tablespoons flour  
½ teaspoon tumeric  
2 tablespoons ground  
  mustard  
1 quart white vinegar  

PROCESS: Cut corn from cob; wipe peppers with damp cloth, cut a slice from stem ends and remove seeds and veins; peel onions. Finely chop cabbage, onions and peppers. Mix well; add one pint vinegar and heat to boiling point. Sift seasonings together twice; add gradually remaining vinegar, stirring constantly; then pour slowly into hot vegetables. Continue cooking thirty-five minutes. Turn into half-pint, sterilized glass jars; seal and store.

# TO DRY CORN

If possible, get the Yellow Bantam green corn. Remove husks and silk. Arrange ears criss-cross in a steamer, cover steamer with a folded crash tea towel, place cover over towel and set steamer over a vessel of boiling water. Steam corn fifteen minutes. Remove from steamer and plunge into very cold water. Drain and with a sharp knife cut corn from the cobs, cutting from the tip toward the butts, using care that corn is not cut so deep as to remove the chaff. With the back of a silver knife scrape the cobs to remove the germ or what is called the "heart of the kernel." Cover small screens or cake coolers with cheese cloth and cover with corn. Do not pile it on too thick, rather strew it over. Place these trays in the oven of the gas range and light the pilot light, turn it half off and leave oven door open; occasionally stir the corn with the hand and alternating the trays in the oven from the top grate to the bottom grate, and one tray may be placed on top of the oven, and at intervals exchanged with those inside. When corn rattles and is readily shaken from the cloth, it is ready to store in tin cans or boxes. Corn may be set in the sun in a screened porch and scattered over larger screens; they must be set indoors when the sun goes down, otherwise the corn will become damp. This is an old-time method but a good one. Small quantities may be dried at a time as soon as green corn is in season.

# TO COOK DRIED CORN

Cover one cup of dried corn with lukewarm water and let it stand over night in a warm place (the back of range is a good place).  In the morning as the water is all absorbed add more water to cover, bring to boiling point and cook slowly until tender (about two hours), add more water if necessary.  Season with salt, pepper and one tablespoon butter and rich milk or thin cream to moisten —about one cup.

# TO CAN SWEET CORN

There is no better corn for canning or general use for that matter than Golden Bantam.  If possible, have the corn fresh pulled from the stalk and husked immediately. Use only the fully developed ears.  With a sharp knife score each row of kernels lengthwise of the ears, with the back of a silver knife press out the heart of pulp leaving the hulls on the cob.  (Be sure that this part of the process is very thoroughly done that there may be no waste). Fill sterilized jars two-thirds full of pulp and no more, as the pulp swells very greatly in the first part of cooking. Fill three jars at a time, place jars in cooker or canner with covers beside them;  cook fifteen minutes, stir down with a silver spoon or knife the corn in each jar, continue stirring at intervals when corn appears to rise to top of jars.  When corn pulp ceases puffing in cooking, then fill two jars to the top from the third and continue cooking thirty minutes.  Wipe tops of jars, adjust rubber rings and covers, do not tightly seal, and finish cooking another half hour.  Seal, remove from canner, cool (out of draft), then store.

# CHAPTER V.

## COLONIAL INDIAN SUET PUDDING

4 cups scalded milk  
1 cup corn meal  
1 cup creamed suet  
1 cup molasses  
2 eggs  
1 teaspoon salt  

½ tablespoon ginger  
½ teaspoon cinnamon  
¾ cup seed and shredded raisins  
2 cups cold milk  
½ cup cold water  

PROCESS: Stir the meal slowly into the milk; add remaining ingredients in the order given, except the cold water and milk; lastly add eggs, beaten thick and light; pour into well buttered baking dish; pour cold water and milk over top (do not stir these into mixture). Bake slowly in a moderate oven three hours. Serve with Hard Sauce or cream and sugar.

## STEAMED INDIAN MEAL PUDDING

1 cup corn meal  
½ cup sour milk  
½ cup N. O. molasses  

⅛ cup finely chopped suet  
1 teaspoon salt  
1 teaspoon ginger  
1 teaspoon soda  

PROCESS: Mix corn meal, molasses, suet and ginger, dissolve soda in sour milk; add to first mixture. Beat well, pour into well buttered mold and steam four hours. Serve with Lemon or Molasses Sauce.

# APPLE AND BROWN BREAD PUDDING

2 cups brown bread crumbs
2 cups chopped apples
⅔ cup finely chopped suet
1 cup seed raisins

½ cup brown sugar
1 egg
2 tablespoons flour
½ teaspoon salt
1 cup milk

PROCESS:  Mix bread crumbs and apple; add suet, raisins mixed with flour and salt; add milk and beat thoroughly.  Steam in buttered molds two hours.  Serve with Lemon or Brandy Sauce.

# INDIAN MEAL PUDDING

1 quart scalded milk
⅛ cup corn meal
2 tablespoons butter
1 cup molasses

1 teaspoon salt
¾ teaspoon cinnamon
¾ teaspoon ginger
2 eggs
1 cup cold milk

PROCESS:  Pour scalded milk slowly on corn meal while stirring constantly and cook in a double boiler twenty minutes, then add butter and molasses.  Sift together salt and spices, add to first mixture; add eggs beaten until thick and lemon tinted.  Turn into a buttered earthen pudding dish and pour cold milk over top. Bake in a slow oven one hour.  Serve with Hard Sauce, top milk or sweetened cream.  The pudding is delicious without sauce.

# BAKED INDIAN PUDDING

5 cups scalded milk

⅛ cup corn meal

½ cup molasses

1 tablespoon butter

1 teaspoon salt

1 teaspoon ginger

PROCESS: Pour hot milk slowly on corn meal. Cook in double boiler twenty-five minutes. Add molasses, butter, salt and sift in the ginger. Turn into a buttered baking dish and bake slowly two hours in a very moderate oven. Serve with Hard Sauce or sweetened cream. If baked too fast it will not whey and will be too solid.

# BAKED INDIAN PUDDING WITH SWEET APPLES

¼ cup corn meal

1 cup cold water

2 cups scalded milk

1 cup molasses

2 eggs

½ teaspoon salt

½ teaspoon ginger

1 teaspoon cinnamon

⅛ teaspoon cloves

4 sweet apples

½ cup cold milk

PROCESS: Pour cold water over corn meal; mix well; then stir gradually into scalded milk, stir until the mixture thickens. Add molasses, eggs beaten until thick and lemon tinted, and salt sifted with spices. Beat thoroughly. Wipe, core, pare and thinly slice apples, put them into a well greased baking dish, pour over the mixture and bake in a moderate oven thirty minutes. Pour over top cold milk and bake without stirring two hours. Serve with top milk or cream.

# BAKED CORN MEAL PUDDING

¼ cup corn meal  
1 cup cold water  
2 cups scalded milk  
½ cup sugar  
2 eggs slightly beaten  

½ cup molasses  
½ teaspoon salt  
1 teaspoon cinnamon  
1 teaspoon ginger  
½ cup milk (extra)  

PROCESS: Stir corn meal into cold milk; add to scalded milk; add sugar, molasses, salt, cinnamon, ginger and egg slightly beaten. Pour into a buttered pudding dish; bake thirty minutes; pour over the extra half cup of cold milk and bake two hours in a moderate oven without stirring.

# BAKED INDIAN MEAL PUDDING
## With Quick Tapioca

¼ cup corn meal  
⅛ cup "quick" tapioca  
1 quart scalded milk  
1 cup molasses  

2 tablespoons butter or  
   butter substitute  
½ teaspoon salt  
1 teaspoon grated orange rind  
½ teaspoon ginger  
1 ½ cups cold milk  

PROCESS: Mix together corn meal and tapioca and sprinkle slowly into hot milk while stirring briskly; stir and cook until tapioca is transparent. Add molasses, butter, salt, orange peel and sift in the ginger. Mix thoroughly and turn into a well greased baking dish. Pour cold milk over top of the mixture and place in the oven without stirring ingredients together. Bake two hours. Serve with or without cream.

## CORN MEAL WITH PEARL TAPIOCA PUDDING

¼ cup corn meal
⅓ cup tapioca soaked in cold
  water over night
4 cups scalded milk
2 tablespoons butter

½ teaspoon salt
½ tablespoon ginger
½ cup seeded and shredded
  raisins
1½ cups cold milk
1 cup molasses

PROCESS: Mix corn meal and tapioca (drained) and stir slowly into scalded milk. Cook in double boiler until tapioca becomes transparent, stirring occasionally; add molasses, salt, ginger, butter and raisins; turn into buttered baking dish. Pour the cold milk over the top; place in oven. Bake one hour; stir once during baking period. Serve with Hard Sauce or Vanilla Sauce.

## INDIVIDUAL CORN MEAL PUDDINGS

Prepare a rule of Hasty Pudding (corn meal mush). Beat three eggs very light, add one cup molasses, two tablespoons melted butter or butter substitute, one teaspoon soda, one-half tablespoon ginger; add sufficient mush to this mixture to make a thick batter. Turn into hissing hot, well greased gem cups to half their depth; press a large seeded raisin into each. Sprinkle top with sugar and cinnamon, add a small dot of butter to each and bake in a hot oven a rich brown. Serve with "Near" Hard Sauce.

# DELICATE INDIAN MEAL PUDDING

4 cups scalded milk  
5 tablespoons corn meal  
4 tablespoons sugar  
1 teaspoon salt  

1 tablespoon butter or  
   butter substitute  
3 eggs  
½ teaspoon ginger  

PROCESS:  Scald milk in double boiler;  add corn meal slowly while stirring briskly;  let cook fifteen minutes, stirring occasionally while cooking;  add salt, sugar and butter;  then remove from range;  add eggs beaten thick and light.  Turn mixture into buttered pudding mold and bake in moderate oven one hour.  Serve with Hard Sauce, "Near" Hard Sauce or sweetened cream.

# INDIAN RICE PUDDING

4 cups scalded milk  
¼ cup rice  
¼ cup Indian meal  

½ cup molasses  
2 tablespoons butter  
½ teaspoon ginger  
½ teaspoon salt  

PROCESS:  Cook the meal in milk in double boiler twenty minutes;  add rice (uncooked), molasses, butter and seasoning.  Pour in buttered pudding dish and bake in moderate oven two hours.  Stir well after cooking one-half hour;  finish cooking without stirring.

# BAKED INDIAN AND APPLE PUDDING

2 cups scalded milk  
¼ cup corn meal  
½ teaspoon salt

½ teaspoon ginger  
¼ cup molasses  
1 tart apple  
Grating orange rind

PROCESS: Pour scalded milk slowly over sifted corn meal while stirring constantly. Cook in double boiler thirty minutes, stirring occasionally. Remove from range, add salt sifted with ginger, molasses and grated orange rind to flavor delicately. Pour into a buttered baking dish and bake slowly one hour in a moderate oven, stirring several times while cooking. Pare, quarter and thinly slice apple and stir into pudding near the last part of cooking. Continue baking until apple is soft. Serve with Molasses Sauce or Hard Sauce.

# DATE CORN MEAL PUDDING

2 cups scalded milk  
½ cup corn meal  
1 tablespoon melted butter or  
  butter substitute

1 cup molasses or sugar  
½ teaspoon cinnamon  
⅔ cup prepared dates  
2 eggs

PROCESS: Pour boiling water over dates; separate them with a fork, drain and dry on a towel at once, remove stones and all the loose skin possible, cut in small pieces. Pour scalded milk over corn meal; add butter, molasses, cinnamon and dates. Beat eggs until thick and lemon tinted and fold into mixture. Turn into a well greased pudding dish and bake until firm or about the consistency of baked custard. Serve with cream or Hard Sauce or "Near" Hard Sauce made of butterine. See "Pudding Sauces."

SKIMMED MILK AND BUTTER SUBSTITUTE MAY BE USED IN ALL
RECIPES EXCEPT THOSE CALLING FOR CREAM.

# CORN MEAL PUDDING WITH COCOANUT

2 tablespoons corn meal
1 tablespoon quick tapioca
2 tablespoons shredded cocoanut
2 cups milk
¼ teaspoon salt
2 tablespoons sugar
1 tablespoon melted butter or butter substitute
⅔ cup molasses

PROCESS: Mix corn meal, tapioca, cocoanut, salt and sugar; add butter, molasses and gradually the milk, stirring constantly. Turn mixture into a well greased pudding dish and bake slowly two hours. Serve plain or with cream.

# IVORY CORNSTARCH PUDDING

2 cups scalded milk
4 tablespoons cornstarch
⅛ teaspoon salt
5 tablespoons sugar
3 egg whites
½ teaspoon vanilla

PROCESS: Mix cornstarch, sugar and salt; add scalded milk, stirring constantly until mixture thickens; cook thirty minutes in double boiler, stirring occasionally. Add the whites of eggs beaten stiff, mix thoroughly, add flavoring. Pour into wet mold, chill and serve with cold sweetened cream.

# GOLDEN CORNSTARCH PUDDING

Follow recipe for Ivory Cornstarch Pudding, substituting yolks of three eggs for the three whites. Flavor with one-fourth teaspoon each of vanilla and lemon extract. Mold, chill and serve.

# CORNSTARCH FRUIT MOLD

Follow recipe for Ivory or Golden Cornstarch Pudding, adding one cup of chopped candied fruits or cooked fruits, drained from their liquor, halves of apricots, sliced peaches, stewed and stoned prunes, to the pudding before molding. If the fruit is in large portions these may be arranged attractively in bottom of wet mold and mixture poured over, pressed into place and chilled thoroughly. Unmold. Serve surrounded with whipped condensed milk or sweetened cream.

# COCOANUT MOLD

Follow recipe for Ivory Cornstarch Pudding, adding one cup freshly grated cocoanut. Mold in individual molds; garnish each with a cherry cut in quarters. Serve with Boiled Custard or whipped cream, sweetened and flavored.

# COCOANUT CONES WITH CHOCOLATE SAUCE

| | |
|---|---|
| 3 tablespoons cornstarch | 2 cups scalded milk |
| 3 tablespoons cold milk | ¾ cup shredded cocoanut |
| 4 tablespoons powdered sugar | Whites 3 eggs |
| ⅛ teaspoon salt | ½ teaspoon vanilla |

PROCESS: Dilute cornstarch with cold milk; add sugar, salt and scalded milk, stirring constantly. Cook in double boiler twenty minutes, continue stirring the first ten minutes of cooking, afterwards occasionally. Add cocoanut; then fold in whites of eggs beaten until stiff. Turn into individual molds previously rinsed with cold water; chill, unmold and serve with Cocoa Sauce.

# COCOA SAUCE

¼ cup sugar  
⅛ teaspoon salt  
Yolks 2 eggs  

1 cup cocoa (powder)  
1 teaspoon butter  
½ teaspoon vanilla  

PROCESS: Sift together the dry ingredients; add yolks slightly beaten and milk gradually while stirring constantly. Cook in double boiler (continue stirring) until mixture coats the spoon. Add vanilla and butter. Serve hot or cold.

# ECONOMICAL CORNSTARCH PUDDING
## Without Eggs

¼ cup cornstarch  
3 tablespoons sugar  
⅛ teaspoon salt  

¼ cup cold skimmed milk  
2 cups scalded skimmed milk  
½ teaspoon vanilla  

PROCESS: Sift together cornstarch, sugar and salt; dilute with cold milk. Add to scalded milk, stirring constantly until mixture thickens, afterwards occasionally. Cook twenty minutes in double boiler. Remove from range, add vanilla. Turn into a mold wet with cold water. Chill. Unmold and serve with Chocolate Sauce.

# HOT CORNSTARCH PUDDING

⅔ cup cornstarch  
¼ cup cold milk  
3¾ cups scalded milk  
¼ teaspoon salt  

¼ cup sugar  
2 eggs  
¼ cup sugar  
½ teaspoon vanilla  

PROCESS: Dilute cornstarch with cold milk; then pour slowly into scalded milk, stirring constantly; add the first portion of sugar and salt, continue stirring until mixture thickens; cover and cook twenty minutes; beat the eggs slightly; add remaining sugar and stir slowly into hot mixture, continue stirring until eggs are thoroughly blended.  Cover and continue cooking three minutes.  Add flavoring and serve hot with sweetened cream.

## ELIZABETH PUDDING

| | |
|---|---|
| 2 cups scalded milk | ⅛ teaspoon salt |
| ¼ cup cornstarch | ¼ cup cold milk |
| ¼ cup sugar | 1 teaspoon lemon or vanilla |
| | Whites 3 eggs |

PROCESS:  Mix sugar, cornstarch and salt; dilute with cold milk; add scalded milk, stirring continually until mixture thickens; cook fifteen minutes.  Flavor; fold in whites of eggs beaten until stiff, mix carefully to retain fluffy consistency; mold; chill and serve with Boiled Custard or Golden Sauce.

## SNOW BALLS WITH CHOCOLATE SAUCE

Follow recipe for Elizabeth Pudding.  Mold in round bottom molds, chill and serve with Chocolate Sauce.

## PINEAPPLE PUDDING

| | |
|---|---|
| 2¾ cups scalded milk | ¼ teaspoon salt |
| ¼ cup cold milk | ½ can finely chopped pine- |
| ⅓ cup cornstarch | apple |
| ⅓ cup sugar | Whites 3 eggs |

PROCESS:  Follow method of making Elizabeth Pudding, adding fruit just before molding.  Fill small fancy molds, first dipped in cold water, chill.  Serve each mold on a circle of canned pineapple; the juice of the pineapple may be thickened slightly and poured over each or whipped cream may be used.

**SKIMMED MILK AND BUTTER SUBSTITUTE MAY BE USED IN ALL RECIPES EXCEPT THOSE CALLING FOR CREAM.**

# REBECCA CORNSTARCH PUDDING

2 cups scalded milk  
⅓ cup cornstarch  
½ cup sugar  
¼ teaspoon salt  
½ cup cold milk

1½ squares chocolate  
3 tablespoons boiling water  
3 whites of eggs  
1 teaspoon vanilla  
½ cup shredded almonds

PROCESS: Mix sugar, cornstarch and salt; dilute with cold milk. Add to scalded milk slowly while stirring constantly; cook fifteen minutes or until mixture thickens. Melt chocolate, add hot water, stir to a smooth paste; add to cooked mixture; add blanched and shredded almonds. Fold in whites of eggs beaten stiff and flavoring. Turn into fancy ring mold wet with cold water. Chill, unmold, fill center with whipped condensed milk.

# CORNSTARCH BLANC MANGE WITH CONDENSED MILK

1 cup condensed milk  
⅓ cup cornstarch  
¼ cup cold water

1 cup boiling water  
¼ teaspoon salt  
½ teaspoon vanilla

PROCESS: Dilute the cornstarch and salt with the cold water. Combine condensed milk with boiling water. Turn into double boiler and slowly pour into hot milk the prepared cornstarch, stirring constantly until mixture thickens, afterwards occasionally. Cook twenty minutes. Turn into individual molds rinsed in cold water; chill, unmold and serve with Boiled Custard.

# CHOCOLATE MOLD

¼ cup cornstarch  
¼ cup sugar  
¼ teaspoon salt  
2 cups scalded milk  

2 squares unsweetened  
   chocolate, melted  
2 tablespoons hot water  
Whites 2 eggs  
½ teaspoon vanilla  

PROCESS: Sift together cornstarch, sugar and salt; add milk gradually, stirring constantly. Melt chocolate, add hot water and cornstarch mixture. Cook over hot water twenty minutes; cool and fold in the whites of eggs beaten until stiff. Add vanilla. Turn into individual molds previously rinsed with cold water. Chill, unmold and serve with sweetened cream.

# ROYAL CHOCOLATE PUDDING

¼ cup cornstarch  
¼ cup sugar  
¼ teaspoon salt  
2 cups milk  

1½ squares chocolate  
2 tablespoons hot water  
Whites 2 eggs  
½ teaspoon vanilla  

PROCESS: Sift together cornstarch, sugar and salt; add to milk, stirring constantly; melt chocolate, add hot water, cornstarch mixture and cook in double boiler thirty minutes; stirring constantly until mixture thickens, afterwards occasionally. Cool, add whites of eggs beaten until stiff, and flavoring. Turn into a mold rinsed with cold water. Chill, unmold and serve with sweetened cream.

# CHERRY FRITTERS

| | |
|---|---|
| ¼ cup cornstarch | ¼ cup cold milk |
| ¼ cup flour | Yolks 2 eggs |
| ½ cup sugar | 2 cups scalded milk |
| ⅛ teaspoon salt | ½ cup Maraschino or candied |
| | cherries finely chopped |

PROCESS: Sift together cornstarch, flour, sugar and salt. Dilute with cold milk; add well beaten yolks of eggs; then add first mixture slowly to scalded milk, stirring constantly, and cook in double boiler fifteen minutes. Remove from range, add cherries and pour in a shallow granite pan rinsed with cold water to the depth of three-fourths of an inch. Chill. Turn on a board, cut in squares, dip in flour, egg and fine cracker crumbs; fry a golden brown in deep, hot fat; drain on brown paper. Serve with Cherry Sauce.

# CHERRY SAUCE

| | |
|---|---|
| 2 tablespoons cornstarch | ¼ cup chopped Maraschino |
| ⅛ cup sugar | cherries |
| ¾ cup boiling water | ½ cup Maraschino syrup |
| | drained from the bottle |
| | 1½ teaspoons butter |

PROCESS: Sift together cornstarch and sugar; add slowly to boiling water, stirring constantly. Boil six minutes, add cherries, syrup and butter. Serve hot with any steamed pudding.

# POPPED CORN PUDDING

3 cups scalded milk
2½ cups popped corn finely
  crushed
3 eggs slightly beaten

½ cup brown sugar
1 tablespoon butter
¾ teaspoon salt
⅔ cup finely chopped pecan
  nut meats

PROCESS: Add scalded milk to prepared popped corn, let stand one hour. Add remaining ingredients in the order given. Turn mixture into a buttered baking dish and bake in a moderate oven until firm. Serve hot with Caramel Sauce or maple syrup or with sweetened cream. Measure popped corn after crushing.

# WHIPPED CREAM SAUCE

1 cup heavy cream

½ cup powdered sugar
½ teaspoon vanilla

PROCESS: Whip cream until stiff, using Dover egg beater. Add sugar and vanilla; chill thoroughly, or follow instructions for whipping condensed milk; use in place of heavy cream.

# TO WHIP CONDENSED MILK

Put a can of condensed milk into a deep saucepan; add water to cover. Place on range and bring to boiling point. Remove can at once from hot water and pour cold water over can to quickly cool milk. Then pack can in ice until thoroughly chilled. Open can and pour the milk into a chilled bowl. Have another larger bowl half filled with crushed ice; place smaller bowl in one containing the ice and stir until milk is chilled; then whip as other cream with a Dover egg beater or a cream whipper. Sweeten and flavor as desired. Place on ice until ready to serve. After following these instructions carefully with the usual satisfactory results condensed milk will be used in this way in the home to a greater extent than ever. Especially at the present extremely high price of "whipping cream."

## CORN MEAL SOUFFLE

3 tablespoons butter
3 tablespoons fine sifted corn
  flour
1 cup milk
Yolks 4 eggs

¼ teaspoon salt
⅓ cup sugar
1 teaspoon grated orange or
  lemon rind
Whites 4 eggs

PROCESS: Melt butter in a saucepan; add corn flour and gradually milk, stirring constantly. Bring to boiling point and cook over boiling water twenty minutes. Remove from range, add yolks of eggs beaten until thick and lemon tinted, mix with lemon or orange rind, salt and sugar. Beat whites of eggs until stiff; then cut and fold them into first mixture. Turn into buttered pudding dish sprinkled with granulated sugar. Place dish in a pan of hot water and bake in a moderate oven about twenty minutes. The water surrounding baking dish should be kept just below the boiling point. The souffle should be well puffed and delicately browned when done. Serve with Whipped Cream Sauce.

## VANILLA SAUCE

½ cup sugar
1 tablespoon cornstarch
⅛ teaspoon salt

1 cup boiling water
2 tablespoons butter
1 teaspoon vanilla extract

PROCESS: Mix and sift sugar and cornstarch; add salt; pour on gradually boiling water, stirring constantly. Simmer ten minutes; remove from range; add butter and vanilla; beat well and serve.

**SKIMMED MILK AND BUTTER SUBSTITUTE MAY BE USED IN ALL RECIPES EXCEPT THOSE CALLING FOR CREAM.**

# LEMON SYRUP

1 cup sugar
¼ cup water

1 teaspoon butter
1 tablespoon lemon juice
A slight grating lemon rind

PROCESS:  Boil water, sugar and lemon peel until it slightly thickens; add butter and lemon juice; beat with gem whip to blend butter; strain and serve at once with waffles or fritters.

# BOILED CUSTARD

2 cups scalded milk
4 egg yolks
⅓ cup sugar

⅛ teaspoon salt
½ tablespoon vanilla

PROCESS:  Beat yolks slightly; add sugar and salt; stir constantly while adding scalded milk slowly.  Cook in double boiler.  Continue stirring until mixture thickens the consistency of thin cream.  Chill and flavor.  Do not allow the water in double boiler to boil vigorously while cooking custard, as this will curdle the custard.  Mixture should form a coating on wooden spoon; it is then cooked sufficiently.

# GOLDEN SAUCE

2 whole eggs
1 egg yolk

1 cup sugar
½ teaspoon vanilla
2 tablespoons sherry

PROCESS:  Beat eggs very light; add sugar gradually; add flavoring and beat thoroughly.

# CHOCOLATE SAUCE

2 cups milk  
1 ½ tablespoons cornstarch  
2 squares chocolate  
¼ cup powdered sugar  

2 tablespoons hot water  
2 eggs  
⅔ cup powdered sugar  
1 teaspoon vanilla  

PROCESS:  Reserve one-fourth cup of milk and scald the remainder.  Dilute cornstarch with cold milk and add to scalded milk.  Cook ten minutes in double boiler, stirring constantly.  Melt chocolate over boiling water;  add one-fourth cup sugar and hot water;  stir to a smooth paste;  add to cooked mixture.  Beat whites of eggs stiff, add powdered sugar slowly and continue beating.  Then add yolks slightly beaten;  add to first mixture.  Cook two minutes;  cool slightly and flavor.

# MOLASSES SAUCE

1 cup Palmetto molasses  
2 tablespoons butter  

2 ½ tablespoons lemon juice  
or malt vinegar  

PROCESS:  Cook molasses and butter together five minutes;  remove from range and add lemon juice or vinegar.

# HARD SAUCE

⅛ cup butter  
1 cup powdered sugar  
½ teaspoon lemon extract  

½ teaspoon vanilla  
Nutmeg  

PROCESS:  Cream butter in earthen bowl with wooden spoon;  add sugar slowly, beating constantly;  add flavoring.  Brandy may be substituted for extracts.  Force mixture through pastry bag with rose tube on a cold plate;  sprinkle with nutmeg;  keep in cool place until ready to serve.

SKIMMED MILK AND BUTTER SUBSTITUTE MAY BE USED IN ALL RECIPES EXCEPT THOSE CALLING FOR CREAM.

# "NEAR" HARD SAUCE

½ cup butterine
1 cup powdered sugar
1 teaspoon vanilla

1 tablespoon brandy
¼ cup whipped condensed
milk or cream

PROCESS: Cream butterine, add sugar slowly, alternately with whipped milk or cream. Add flavoring slowly also while beating constantly. Serve very cold. See Page 106, "To Whip Condensed Milk."

## APPLE SAUCE
### For Puddings

1 cup chopped apple
1 tablespoon cornstarch
Few grains salt
½ cup cold water

1 tablespoon lemon juice
Grated rind ½ lemon
Cinnamon
Sugar

PROCESS: Sift cornstarch over apples, add salt, cold water, lemon juice and rind. Add cinnamon and sugar to taste. Cook ten minutes. Rub through a sieve and serve hot with steamed puddings.

## APRICOT SAUCE

½ cup apricot pulp or
  1 cup apricot juice
½ cup sugar

½ cup orange juice or water
1 teaspoon cornstarch
1 tablespoon lemon juice
Few grains salt

PROCESS: Mix ingredients in the order given and boil gently ten minutes, stirring constantly. Strain through coarse sieve and serve with hot puddings, dumplings, etc.

# "ITALIA" SAUCE

| | |
|---|---|
| 2 tablespoons butter | ½ cup boiling water |
| 1 cup powdered sugar | Juice and grated rind 1 lemon |
| ½ tablespoon cornstarch | ½ cup finely shredded |
| Few grains salt | Angelica or citron |
| Yolks 3 eggs slightly beaten | ½ cup candied cherries finely cut |

PROCESS: Cream butter, add half the sugar and cornstarch sifted together. Add remaining sugar to beaten egg yolks; combine mixtures; add boiling water slowly, stirring constantly. Cook three minutes, continue stirring. Add remaining ingredients, bring to boiling point and serve with steamed fruit, suet or plum pudding.

# CHAPTER VI.

## CORNSTARCH CAKE

¾ cup butter or butter substitute
2 cups fine cake sugar
1 cup milk
1 cup cornstarch

2 cups flour
4½ teaspoons baking powder
Whites 5 eggs
½ teaspoon each lemon and
  vanilla extract

PROCESS: Cream the butter with a wooden spoon in an earthen mixing bowl; add sugar gradually; sift cornstarch, flour, salt and baking powder together twice; add alternately to first mixture with milk; lastly cut and fold in the whites of eggs beaten until stiff; add extract. Turn mixture into two brick-shaped bread pans, buttered and floured. Bake forty-five minutes in moderate oven. Frost with boiled frosting or serve without frosting.

## BOILED FROSTING

1 cup granulated sugar
⅛ teaspoon cream tartar

¼ cup cold water
1 egg white beaten stiff
¼ teaspoon vanilla extract

PROCESS: Mix well, sugar, cream tartar and cold water in a saucepan, place on range, bring to boiling point, stirring constantly until sugar is dissolved; then cook without stirring until the syrup drops from wooden spoon like honey. Remove from range, add three table-spoons of syrup to the white of egg, beating constantly until well blended; return remaining syrup to range and cook until it will spin a thread; remove from range at once and pour syrup in a fine stream into first mixture.

Continue beating, add vanilla. Beat until frosting cools slightly and begins to glaze on sidea of pan. Pour on cake, spread evenly, let cool before cutting cake.

## BOSTON VELVET CAKE

½ cup butter or butter substitute
1 ½ cups fine granulated sugar
Yolks 4 eggs
½ cup cold water
1 ¼ cups flour
½ cup cornstarch

4 teaspoons baking powder
⅛ teaspoon salt
Whites 4 eggs
½ teaspoon almond extract
½ cup blanched and shredded almonds

PROCESS: Cream butter, add sugar gradually, yolks of eggs beaten very light and water. Sift the flour, cornstarch, salt and baking powder; add to first mixture. Lastly, cut and fold in the whites of eggs beaten stiff; add extract; turn mixture into a buttered and floured, shallow cake pan. Sprinkle almonds over the top of cake. Bake thirty-five minutes in a moderate oven. Do not frost this cake.

# ANGEL FOOD WITH CORNSTARCH

1 cup white of eggs  
1 cup fine granulated sugar  
¾ cup pastry flour  

¼ cup cornstarch  
½ teaspoon cream of tartar  
1 teaspoon vanilla extract  

PROCESS:  Beat whites of eggs until foamy;  add cream of tartar and beat until stiff and dry;  add sugar gradually while beating constantly;  add vanilla;  then cut and fold in flour and cornstarch previously sifted together five times.  Turn into an unbuttered angel food pan.  Bake in a slow oven from thirty to fifty minutes, according to the size of the pan.  Invert pan on a cake cooler and allow cake to cool, loosen and fall out.

## LITTLE QUEENS

½ cup shortening (butter)  
Grated rind 1 lemon  
1 cup sugar  
Yolks 4 eggs  
2 tablespoons lemon juice  

1 cup pastry flour  
¼ cup sifted corn flour  
¼ teaspoon salt  
¼ teaspoon soda  
Whites 4 eggs  

PROCESS:  Cream shortening;  add sugar gradually and continue stirring.  Then add grated rind, lemon juice and yolks of eggs, beaten until thick and lemon tinted.  Sift together flours, salt and soda;  add to first mixture and beat thoroughly.  Then cut and fold in the whites of eggs beaten until stiff.  Fill small buttered muffin tins two-thirds full of mixture and bake twenty to twenty-five minutes in a hot oven.

# WAR TIME DROP CAKES

¼ cup shortening (chicken fat)  
1 cup sugar  
1 egg well beaten  
Grated rind 1 orange  
¼ cup strained orange juice  

1 ¼ cup pastry flour  
¾ cup corn flour  
¼ teaspoon salt  
4 teaspoons baking powder  
¼ cup shredded citron or  
⅛ cup chopped nut meats  

PROCESS: Cream shortening; add sugar gradually while stirring constantly. Add egg beaten until thick and lemon tinted, grated rind and orange juice. Sift together flour, corn flour, salt and baking powder. Add citron or nut meats, then stir into first mixture. Mix well. Drop by teaspoonfuls one and one-half inches apart on a well greased baking sheet and bake twelve to fifteen minutes in a hot oven. When eggs are plentiful add another one to mixture.

# CORN MEAL DOUGHNUTS

1 cup fine corn meal or corn flour  
¾ cup white flour  
½ cup sugar  
¼ teaspoon salt  
½ teaspoon nutmeg  

½ teaspoon soda  
½ cup sour milk  
1 tablespoon melted shortening  
1 egg  
Flour  

PROCESS: Heat milk and pour it over corn meal; add melted shortening, sugar, salt and nutmeg. Sift soda with flour, add to first mixture, beat thoroughly, then fold in the egg beaten until thick and lemon tinted; add sufficient flour to make a soft dough. Chill dough, then roll to one-half-inch thickness and shape with a doughnut cutter. Fry in deep, hot fat. Drain on brown paper, when cool dredge with powdered sugar.

# CORNSTARCH CREAM PUFFS

½ cup butter     1 cup cornstarch
1 cup milk      4 eggs

PROCESS:  Bring half of the milk to boiling point; add butter and when melted stir in cornstarch diluted with remaining milk.  Stir vigorously until mixture is smooth.  Remove from range and add unbeaten eggs, one at a time, beating until thoroughly blended between the addition of eggs.  Drop by spoonfuls (the size of a small egg) on a buttered sheet one and one-half inches apart, shaping with the handle of a wooden spoon in circles, having each slightly piled in center.  Bake thirty minutes in a moderate oven.  With a thin sharp knife make a cut in the side of each puff large enough to admit of cream filling.  This recipe will make one and one-half dozen cakes.  If cream cakes are removed from oven before being baked through they will fall.  If in doubt, remove one from the sheet and it if does not fall it is sufficient evidence that the others are baked throughout.

## CREAM FILLING

¾ cup sugar     2 eggs
4 tablespoons cornstarch  1 egg yolk
⅛ teaspoon salt    2 cups scalded milk
          1 teaspoon vanilla

PROCESS:  Mix the dry ingredients; add eggs and egg yolk slightly beaten and pour on slowly scalded milk while stirring constantly, until mixture thickens, afterwards occasionally.  Cook fifteen minutes, cool and add vanilla.  Use as filling between layers of cake as for Cream Cakes.

# POPPED CORN MACAROONS

¾ cup finely chopped popped
  corn
¾ tablespoon melted butter
White 1 egg
5 ½ tablespoons sugar

¼ teaspoon salt
½ teaspoon vanilla
Blanched and finely chopped
  almonds
Candied cherries

PROCESS:  Add butter to corn;  beat white of egg until stiff;  add sugar gradually;  continue beating.  Add to first mixture;  add salt and vanilla.  Drop from tip of teaspoon on a well buttered baking sheet one and one-half inches apart.  With the spoon shape in circles and flatten with a knife, first dipped in cold water.  Sprinkle with chopped nut meats and press a shred of candied cherry in top of each macaroon.  Bake in a slow oven until daintily browned.

## CORN FLAKE KISSES

Beat two eggs until thick and lemon tinted;  add gradually one cup sugar, beating constantly.  Add two and three-fourths cups corn flakes and one cup chopped nut meats, mix thoroughly.  Add a sprinkle of salt. Drop in generous teaspoonfuls in rounds on a buttered cooky sheet one and one-half inches apart.  Bake twenty minutes in a slow oven.  Maple flakes are sometimes used in place of the plain corn flakes.

**SKIMMED MILK AND BUTTER SUBSTITUTE MAY BE USED IN ALL RECIPES EXCEPT THOSE CALLING FOR CREAM.**

# POPCORN BRITTLE

3 cups brown sugar
1 cup N. O. molasses
½ teaspoon cream tartar
½ cup butter or butter
substitute
2 teaspoons soda
2 tablespoons hot water
1 quart freshly popped corn

PROCESS: Boil the first three ingredients in an iron kettle to the "hard crack" degree (310 degrees F.), i. e., when a little of the syrup is dropped into ice water it will form a hard ball and when pressed between the teeth it will not stick, but will leave them clean and free from taffy; add butter and when it is well blended add popcorn; stir it well. Remove from range, add soda dissolved in hot water, stir briskly; when mixture begins to rise turn it on an oiled or butter marble slab or platter; spread thin and evenly; when cold break in small pieces.

# POPCORN BARS

1 quart freshly popped corn
1 cup sugar
¼ cup corn syrup
¼ cup water
1 tablespoon butterine or butter
1 teaspoon salt

PROCESS: Carefully pick over fresh popped corn, discarding all unpopped kernels. Pass through meat-chopper, using coarse knife; sprinkle with salt. Into a kettle put sugar, prepared corn and water; cook until candy cracks when tested in cold water (about 270 degrees F., on sugar thermometer). Add butter and cook until candy is very hard when again tested in cold water (ice-water is preferable). Add corn, stir until thoroughly blended. Return to range to warm slightly and pour on an oiled marble slab or an enameled tray and with a slightly oiled rolling-pin roll as thin as possible. (This operation must be done quickly.) Cut in bars or squares. If it becomes too hard to cut break in small pieces.

# MAPLE POPCORN BALLS

3 quarts freshly popped corn  
1 cup melted maple sugar  
Salt  

½ cup brown sugar  
1 tablespoon butter or butterine  

PROCESS: Carefully pick over popped corn, discarding all unpopped kernels. Melt butter or butterine in a large, round-bottom, iron kettle (an old-fashioned type if one is available); a large granite kettle will serve the purpose. Add maple syrup and sugar; bring to boiling point and cook until mixture will crack when tested in cold water. Sprinkle corn with salt; pour candy slowly over prepared popped corn while stirring briskly. Shape with slightly buttered hands quickly and little pressure into balls. When cool wrap in waxed paper. To prepare maple sugar, shave or break in small pieces, then measure. To one cup sugar add one-half cup of water and cook until the consistency of syrup. This will be found more satisfactory than commercial maple syrup, notwithstanding the extra trouble.

# POPCORN BALLS

1½ cups sugar  
5½ tablespoons glucose  
⅔ cup water  
½ cup (good) molasses  

2 tablespoons butterine  
½ teaspoon salt  
5 quarts freshly popped corn  

PROCESS: Into a kettle put sugar, glucose and water; stir until sugar is melted; wash down sides of kettle, cover and cook gently five minutes; uncover and cook without stirring until when a little is tested in cold water it will crack (about 275 to 280 degrees F.). Add remaining ingredients except popped corn and continue cooking until very brittle when again tested in cold water.   Stir occasionally at first then, constantly. Carefully pick over corn, discarding all unpopped kernels. Put corn in a hot mixing bowl slightly buttered, sprinkle with salt and stir briskly while pouring the taffy over it. Mix well, then roll in balls with as little pressure as possible.   Pile in a pyramid on a buttered platter.

## PARCHED SWEET CORN

2 cups sweet seed corn       Salt
4 tablespoons butter or olive oil     Boiling water

PROCESS:  Pick over corn, removing all imperfect kernels and bits of cob.  Put corn in sieve and pour boiling water over it.  Drain on crash towel.  Melt butter in iron spider, add corn and stir constantly until each kernel is delicately browned and puffed.  Drain on brown paper, sprinkle with salt.  Shake corn in a coarse sieve to get ride of superfluous salt.  Serve same as salted nuts. If one cup of corn is parched at a time it will brown more evenly.

## PLEASE READ THESE BULLETINS
### (They will prove very valuable to you)

Farmer's Bulletin No. 565.   U. S. Dept. Agr. Corn Meal as a Food and Ways of Using.   By C. F. Langworthy and Caroline Hunt.

Farmer's Bulletin No. 298.   Printed in 1907—Food Value of Corn and Corn Products.   By Charles D. Woods, D. Sc., Director of Maine Agricultural Experiment Station.

The latter bulletin will prove invaluable to those who are especially interested in teaching Household Economics—which includes Thrift and Conservation of Food.

**SKIMMED MILK AND BUTTER SUBSTITUTE MAY BE USED IN ALL RECIPES EXCEPT THOSE CALLING FOR CREAM.**

# MEMORANDUM

---

# MEMORANDUM

---

**Bread**—Alabama Pumpkin Corn...........................  57
    Blueberry Corn...................  .......  65
    Boston Brown...........  ...........  ...........  46
    Boston Brown with Fruit  .  ...  ...........  ...........  47
    Corn, with Creamed Clams  ........  ...  ..  65
    Corn (New Orleans Recipe) .  ......  ........  54
    Corn Meal and Graham...  .  ........  ...........  51
    Corn Meal Date............  .  ....  ...  ....  48
    Crackling Corn Bread....  ..  ..  ...........  56
    Creamed Corn...........  ..  ...........  54
    "Delicia" Corn Meal and Brown Rice Griddle Cakes.  ....  31
    Eggless Corn, No. 1.......  .  ...........  ..  59
    Eggless Corn, No. 2..........  .  ...........  ..  59
    Indian Meal (with yeast)....  .  ....  ....  50
    Indian Meal and Rye Meal . .  ..........  ..  49
    Kentucky Spoon Corn.......  .  ...  ...........  62
    Knoxville Corn.................  ...........  56
    Molasses Corn...........  .  ...........  58
    Old Fashioned Corn (Southern Recipe).....  ...........  55
    Old Virginia Batter...................  60
    Pone Corn.......................  15
    Quick War Bread...................  46
    Raised Brown Bread, No. 2.....  ...........  50
    Rice and Corn Meal Spoon...  ...........  62
    South Carolina Spoon Corn Bread ....  ...  ...........  53
    Southern Corn...................  53
    Steamed Brown...................  47
    Sweet Corn...................  55
    Thin Corn...................  ...........  58
    Virginia Spoon Corn....  .  ...  ...........  63
    White Corn Meal .....  .  ...........  58
**Cakes**—Angel Food with Cornstarch  ...........  114
    Apple Johnny...........  .  ...........  64
    Boston Velvet................  ..  ...........  113
    Cornstarch...................  ...........  112
    Custard Corn...................  63
    Flannel, No. 1...................  34
    Flannel, No. 2.................  35
    Luncheon Johnny...................  64
    Rhode Island Johnny.....  ...........  17
    Sour Milk Corn....  ...........  30
    Sponge Corn, No. 1. ......  .  ...........  60
    Sponge Corn, No. 2...........  ...........  60
    Spider Corn...................  57
    Virginia Corn...................  76
    War Time Drop....  ...........  115
**Chowder**—Corn......  ...........  87
**Cones**—Cocoanut with Chocolate Sauce....  ...........  100
**Corn and Bacon**...................  84
**Corn a la Mexican** ....  ...  ...........  71
**Corn Croquettes**.....  ...........  79

Corn Flake Kisses...................................... 117
Corn Meal for Crumbing Fish........................... 26
Corn Oysters.......................................... 75
Corn Relish........................................... 89
Corn Southern Style................................... 71
Corn Timbales......................................... 79
Corn Toast............................................ 84
Corn with Cream....................................... 67
Corn Sticks........................................... 28
Cornstarch Blanc Mange with Condensed Milk............ 103
Cornstarch Cream Puffs................................ 116
Cream Corn Meal Gems.................................. 24
Creamed Corn au Gratin................................ 78
Crispys, Corn Meal.................................... 17
Custard—Boiled........................................ 108
  Corn................................................ 80
  Kornlet............................................. 80
Dodgers—Corn Meal, No. 1.............................. 14
  Corn Meal, No. 2.................................... 15
Doughnuts—Corn Meal................................... 115
Fritters—Cherry....................................... 105
  Corn and Celery..................................... 74
  Corn and Oyster..................................... 75
  Corn, No. 1......................................... 73
  Corn, No. 2......................................... 73
  Sweet Corn, No. 3................................... 74
Frosting—Boiled....................................... 112
  Creamed Filling..................................... 116
Gnocchi a la Romaine.................................. 42
Gnocchi au Gratin..................................... 43
Griddle Cakes—Corn Meal and Buckwheat................. 33
  Corn Meal and Rice (Sour Milk)...................... 30
  Corn Meal and Rice (Sweet Milk)..................... 31
  Corn Meal, No. 1.................................... 32
  Corn Meal, No. 2.................................... 29
  Green Corn, No. 1................................... 83
  Green Corn, No. 2................................... 83
  Hominy.............................................. 36
  Left Over Granulated Hominy......................... 34
  "Pete's" Corn Meal.................................. 33
  Scalded Corn Meal................................... 32
Green Corn—Boiled..................................... 66
  Au Gratin........................................... 78
  Cooked in Milk...................................... 66
  Creole.............................................. 69
  Fried............................................... 68
  Green Peppers Stuffed with.......................... 77
  New England Style (Sweet Corn)...................... 72
  Parched Sweet Corn.................................. 120
  Roasted............................................. 66
  Scrambled with Eggs................................. 82
  Soup................................................ 86
  Steamed, on the Cob................................. 67

**Green Corn—Continued**
  Stewed........................................................ 68
  Tomatoes Stuffed with......................................... 76
  To Can Sweet Corn............................................. 91
  To Cook Dried Corn............................................ 91
  To Dry Corn................................................... 90
  To Sweeten Green Corn When Boiling............................ 67
  Waffles....................................................... 82
**Hash**—Corn................................................... 89
**Hominy**—Casserole of, with Meat............................. 42
  Granulated Hominy Crusts ..................................... 37
  With Horse-Radish Croquettes.................................. 38
  Balls......................................................... 38
  Boulettes..................................................... 41
  Croquettes.................................................... 37
  Crusts........................................................ 43
  Puff.......................................................... 40
  Waffles, No. 1................................................ 35
  Waffles, No. 2................................................ 36
  With Tomatoes................................................. 39
  Pearl, with Minced Ham........................................ 39
  Savory........................................................ 37
  Steamed Pearl................................................. 13
**Indian Bannocks**............................................. 16
**Indian Meal Flapjacks**....................................... 17
**Jolly Joe**................................................... 48
**Little Queens**............................................... 114
**Mold**—Chocolate............................................. 104
  Cocoanut...................................................... 100
  Cornstarch Fruit ............................................. 100
  Mammy's Pumpkin .............................................. 61
**Muffins**—Corn Meal and Barley Meal.......................... 26
  Corn Meal and Rice............................................ 24
  Corn Meal, No. 1.............................................. 22
  Corn Meal, No. 2.............................................. 22
  Corn Meal with Rice........................................... 23
  Cream Corn.................................................... 24
  Currant....................................................... 23
  Dainty Corn Meal.............................................. 25
  Fried Corn Meal............................................... 49
  Hominy and Corn Meal.......................................... 27
  Hominy........................................................ 28
  Raised Corn................................................... 51
  Rich Corn Meal................................................ 25
**Mush**—Corn Meal with Lemon Flavor........................... 12
  Fried Corn Meal............................................... 11
  Fried, Fairmont Style......................................... 12
**Norfolk Waffles**............................................. 36
**Omelet**—Corn................................................ 81
**Paunhaus**.................................................... 13
**Philadelphia Scrapple**....................................... 20

**Polenta**—with Cheese . . . . . . . . . . . . . . . . . . . . . . . . . . . . . . . . 19
    With Mushroom Sauce. . . . . . . . . . . . . . . . . . . . . . . . . . . . . 18
    Spanish. . . . . . . . . . . . . . . . . . . . . . . . . . . . . . . . . . . . . . . . 19
**Pone**—Corn Bread. . . . . . . . . . . . . . . . . . . . . . . . . . . . . . . . . . . 15
    Corn. . . . . . . . . . . . . . . . . . . . . . . . . . . . . . . . . . . . . . . . . . 61
    Onion Corn. . . . . . . . . . . . . . . . . . . . . . . . . . . . . . . . . . . . . 20
**Popovers**—Corn Meal. . . . . . . . . . . . . . . . . . . . . . . . . . . . . . . . 26
**Poppets**. . . . . . . . . . . . . . . . . . . . . . . . . . . . . . . . . . . . . . . . . . 28
**Popcorn**—Maple Balls. . . . . . . . . . . . . . . . . . . . . . . . . . . . . . . 119
    Balls. . . . . . . . . . . . . . . . . . . . . . . . . . . . . . . . . . . . . . . . . . 119
    Bars. . . . . . . . . . . . . . . . . . . . . . . . . . . . . . . . . . . . . . . . . . 118
    Brittle. . . . . . . . . . . . . . . . . . . . . . . . . . . . . . . . . . . . . . . . . 118
    Macaroons. . . . . . . . . . . . . . . . . . . . . . . . . . . . . . . . . . . . . 117
**Pudding**—Apple and Brown Bread. . . . . . . . . . . . . . . . . . . . . . 93
    Baked Corn Meal. . . . . . . . . . . . . . . . . . . . . . . . . . . . . . . . 95
    Baked Indian and Apple. . . . . . . . . . . . . . . . . . . . . . . . . . . 98
    Baked Indian Meal. . . . . . . . . . . . . . . . . . . . . . . . . . . . . . . 95
    Baked Indian. . . . . . . . . . . . . . . . . . . . . . . . . . . . . . . . . . . 94
    Baked Indian, with Sweet Apples. . . . . . . . . . . . . . . . . . . . 94
    Colonial Indian Suet. . . . . . . . . . . . . . . . . . . . . . . . . . . . . . 92
    Corn Meal with Pearl Tapioca . . . . . . . . . . . . . . . . . . . . . . 96
    Corn Meal with Cocoanut. . . . . . . . . . . . . . . . . . . . . . . . . . 99
    Corn Meal Yorkshire. . . . . . . . . . . . . . . . . . . . . . . . . . . . . . 29
    Corn. . . . . . . . . . . . . . . . . . . . . . . . . . . . . . . . . . . . . . . . . . 82
    Date Corn Meal . . . . . . . . . . . . . . . . . . . . . . . . . . . . . . . . . 98
    Delicate Indian Meal. . . . . . . . . . . . . . . . . . . . . . . . . . . . . . 97
    Economical Cornstarch (without Eggs). . . . . . . . . . . . . . . 101
    Elizabeth. . . . . . . . . . . . . . . . . . . . . . . . . . . . . . . . . . . . . . 102
    Golden Cornstarch. . . . . . . . . . . . . . . . . . . . . . . . . . . . . . . 99
    Green Corn . . . . . . . . . . . . . . . . . . . . . . . . . . . . . . . . . . . . . 81
    Hasty. . . . . . . . . . . . . . . . . . . . . . . . . . . . . . . . . . . . . . . . . 11
    Hot Cornstarch . . . . . . . . . . . . . . . . . . . . . . . . . . . . . . . . . 101
    Indian Meal. . . . . . . . . . . . . . . . . . . . . . . . . . . . . . . . . . . . 93
    Indian Rice . . . . . . . . . . . . . . . . . . . . . . . . . . . . . . . . . . . . 97
    Individual Corn Meal. . . . . . . . . . . . . . . . . . . . . . . . . . . . . 96
    Ivory Cornstarch. . . . . . . . . . . . . . . . . . . . . . . . . . . . . . . . 99
    Pineapple . . . . . . . . . . . . . . . . . . . . . . . . . . . . . . . . . . . . . 102
    Popped Corn . . . . . . . . . . . . . . . . . . . . . . . . . . . . . . . . . . . 106
    Rebecca Cornstarch . . . . . . . . . . . . . . . . . . . . . . . . . . . . . 103
    Royal Chocolate . . . . . . . . . . . . . . . . . . . . . . . . . . . . . . . 104
    Steamed Indian Meal. . . . . . . . . . . . . . . . . . . . . . . . . . . . . 92
**Rolls**—Parker House Corn. . . . . . . . . . . . . . . . . . . . . . . . . . . . 27
    Raised Corn Flour Parker House . . . . . . . . . . . . . . . . . . . 52
**Salad**—Corn . . . . . . . . . . . . . . . . . . . . . . . . . . . . . . . . . . . . . . 88
    Corn and Tomato . . . . . . . . . . . . . . . . . . . . . . . . . . . . . . . 88
**Samp**—au Gratin. . . . . . . . . . . . . . . . . . . . . . . . . . . . . . . . . . . 40
    Steamed . . . . . . . . . . . . . . . . . . . . . . . . . . . . . . . . . . . . . . 14
**Sauces**—Apple for Puddings . . . . . . . . . . . . . . . . . . . . . . . . . . 110
    Apricot . . . . . . . . . . . . . . . . . . . . . . . . . . . . . . . . . . . . . . . 110
    Bechamel. . . . . . . . . . . . . . . . . . . . . . . . . . . . . . . . . . . . . . 44
    Cheese. . . . . . . . . . . . . . . . . . . . . . . . . . . . . . . . . . . . . . . . 45
    Cherry. . . . . . . . . . . . . . . . . . . . . . . . . . . . . . . . . . . . . . . . 105

**Sauces—Continued**
    Chocolate......................................... 109
    Cocoa............................................ 101
    Golden........................................... 108
    Hard............................................. 109
    "Italia"......................................... 111
    Molasses......................................... 109
    Mushroom......................................... 18
    "Near" Hard...................................... 110
    Thin White....................................... 41
    Tomato........................................... 44
    Vanilla.......................................... 107
    Whipped Cream.................................... 106
**Scalloped Corn**....................................... 72
**Scrapple with Liver Sausage**......................... 21
**Snow Balls with Chocolate Sauce**..................... 103
**Souffle—Corn Meal**................................... 107
**Soup—Corn with Tomatoes**............................. 86
    Corn with Whipped Cream.......................... 85
    Cream of Corn.................................... 85
    Green Corn....................................... 86
**Steamed Corn Meal**................................... 47
**Stewed Corn and Tomatoes**............................ 73
**Substitutes to use for Buttering Crumbs**............. 45
**Succotash**........................................... 69
    With Tomatoes.................................... 70
    Tomatoes Stuffed with............................ 77
    Southern......................................... 70
**Syrup—Lemon**......................................... 108
**To Whip Condensed Milk**.............................. 106